The Man of Galilee

Atticus G. Haygood

DEWARD
PUBLISHING COMPANY

The Man of Galilee
DeWard Publishing Company, Ltd.
P.O. Box 6259, Chillicothe, Ohio 45601
www.deward.com

Printed in the United States of America.

The text for this edition was taken from Ferrell Jenkins' Biblical Studies Info Page **(biblicalstudies.info)**. It is reprinted here with permission. *The Man of Galilee* is in the public domain. No rights reserved.

ISBN: 978-0-9798893-1-8

To the "Emory Boys,"
Who were with me in the Old College in 1876–84,
this little book is dedicated by one who loves them all.

The Author
Decatur, Ga.,
April 9, 1889

PREFATORY

The Rev. Lundy H. Harris,
Professor in Emory College, Oxford, Ga.

My Dear Lundy:

You and many others of my students at Emory of the years 1876–1884 have often asked me to put into permanent form the thoughts concerning "The Man of Galilee"—"Jesus of Nazareth"—I brought before you when we were together at the old college in Oxford. In this little book I have had the boys in mind all the way through, as if they were before me in my lecture-room in "Seney Hall." Many times the very faces of the boys seemed to be about me as I have written, and I could almost hear them ask me questions as they used to do.

Scattered about the world now—not a few of them in distant mission fields—my heart follows them every one, and these pages, which would never have appeared but for them, bear them the assurance of an interest in them that can never die.

Your friend,

Atticus G. Haygood

CONTENTS

1963 Preface

About thirty-five years ago, while a student in college, one of my professors let me read his copy of *The Man of Galilee*, by A. G. Haygood. I was so impressed with the simple argument made by the author, as he took the Gospel story of Jesus and showed the evidence of His deity, that I sought until I found a copy for myself and copies for the libraries of the schools in which I have taught.

The reader will find the book interesting, factual, and logically arranged, as the author builds his case for the supernatural Christ. He presents Jesus as His own evidence to His deity.

I have long wished that someone would bring out a reprint of this excellent work; and I take pleasure in commending Mr. Jenkins for satisfying this desire. I heartily recommend the book to all who are in search of a simple presentation of Jesus Himself as evidence to His deity.

Homer Hailey
Temple Terrace, Florida
May, 1963

It is with pleasure and satisfaction that we present the reprint of *The Man of Galilee*. Nearly since the beginning of the publication of *Evidence Quarterly* we have had this in mind. We have had an admiration for the books since being introduced to it by Homer Hailey in one of his classes on the Evidences of Christianity.

In establishing the deity of Jesus there is no fact more outstanding and no stone more solid than Jesus Himself as presented by the Gospel records. Mr. Haygood caught something of the power and beauty of the original argument and recorded it for us in *The Man of Galilee*.

While we do not agree with every illustration and conclusion of the author we thought it best not to cumber his work with our notes; as a whole the work is excellent. It is our prayer in reprinting it that readers may be drawn to a closer study of the Gospelas and to a great appreciation of Him who is Truth.

Ferrell Jenkins
Bowling Green, Kentucky
June, 1963

NEW PREFACE

My first introduction to Atticus G. Haygood's The Man of Galilee was in a class on Evidences of Christianity taught by Ferrell Jenkins, who assigned it as required reading. In my estimation the argument for the deity of Jesus Christ based upon the gospel account of his life is among the most convincing that can be offered.

Haygood discusses the truly unique and universal quality of the character of Jesus in a manner that is thoughtful, thorough, and logical. It is presented in terms that the student will find interesting, refreshing, and in the end, compelling. As with so many generations of Bible students who have gone before, today's students can still be enriched by a careful reading of this book on the life of the man who himself is the way, the truth, and the life.

I wish to thank DeWard Publishing Company for undertaking the task of producing another reprint of this timeless work. May all who read it be impressed with the grand, unequalled character of Jesus and may their faith in his deity be made stronger.

Daniel W. Petty
Temple Terrace, Florida
April, 2008

1

DID THE EVANGELISTS INVENT JESUS?

Who and what was Jesus of Nazareth? In this question and its answer is involved the whole of what we mean by Christianity.

If it could be demonstrably proved that there never existed such a person as Jesus, Christianity, as a living force, would cease from the earth. There would indeed be a history, a literature that would interest people according to their tastes; but there would be no heart-changing, world-up-lifting system of vital and vitalizing truths and corresponding duties, binding upon the conscience of every human being and inspiring hope in every breast.

In the discussions we are about to enter nothing will be assumed except what is too obvious to question. It will not be assumed that the little books called "gospels" were inspired at all. You will not be asked to consider any miracle, said to have been performed by Jesus, as making proof of his divinity. Nor will I quote proof-texts to show that he is divine.

The first question to ask is this: Did such a person as Jesus is described to have been ever really exist? Did Jesus really live in Nazareth and work in Joseph's shop? Did he, for some three years and six months, go to and fro among men teaching them? Was there, in the days of Herod and Pilate, a Jesus as surely as there was a Caesar?

This much is certain. we have in these four little books—compared with what is every day written about common men how small they are!—attributed to Matthew, Mark, Luke, and John, a most distinct character, known to us and known to history as Jesus. Whether the men whose names the little books bear, or some other men whose names are lost to us wrote them, matters not in the least. What books contain is more important than the question of authorship. No matter who wrote them, the character we know as Jesus is in the books; there can be no dispute about this; here it is, before our eyes. And this character is as surely in history, in literature, in men's thoughts, in all that we mean by Christian civilization, as it is in the writings of the four men we call evangelists.

Not only do we have the character, but we see clearly that it is a character absolutely unique. It is unique in many respects, but pre-eminently in this—it is the one perfect character that has appeared in the world that ever had a place in the history or the thought of men. It is said that the volatile Voltaire once compared Jesus to Fletcher of Madeley, thinking him as good a man as the Nazarene. But the light Frenchman understood neither the one nor the other. As one said of an unfit biographer of Fletcher's great friend, John Wesley: "He had nothing to draw with, and the well was deep."

Is there one solitary defect, the very least, in this character that we find in the evangelists? Is there one weak spot, or suggestion of fault, or intimation of infirmity, or suspicion of failure, the slightest, to do and to be what was right for him to do and to be?

Look at him as he is set before us in these brief writings; look, reverently if you will, but with open and fearless eyes, to see all that may be seen of him. What least flaw can be found in him? Is there the least possible shadow of reason for reversing, or so much as questioning, Pilate's verdict, "I find no fault in him?" Is there in all history one other character of which you can say or believe as much? Is there any other you are willing to name second to him?

If you are making an estimate of any other character—whether of a real person, as a sage, a statesman, or a philanthropist, or of some imaginary person, as the hero of a story—how would you judge him most severely? You would compare him with Jesus. We must remember that it is to Jesus we owe those higher standards by which we judge men in our times. Christ-likeness expresses the highest ideal of character we are capable of conceiving.

Some writers, as you know, have denied that Jesus, the Jesus of the four gospels, did at any time really live, a man among men. Of far more importance than any mere denials in books is the failure of many thousands to realize in their inmost consciousness that the story of the evangelists is the record of a life actually lived.

We will demand of those who deny or doubt that Jesus really lived to account to us for the existence of the character. This they must do, for the existence of the character they cannot deny; it is here before men's eyes, as it is in men's thoughts and lives. This character is not in these little books only; it is in a hundred thousand books. It was not only in the minds of four writers long ago; it is in the minds of millions of men, women, and children today. If any deny or doubt the historic Jesus, let them explain to us how this character, flawless and perfect, ever got itself into the thoughts of men and now in history, literature, art, law, custom, in human life itself.

Some have tried to explain the existence of the character, while denying that Jesus really lived among men, by telling us the evangelists invented the Jesus of these stories. They tell us Jesus is the product of the dramatic genius of the four men whose names go with the brief account we have of him, his words, and his deeds. It would not alter the case to deny that these four wrote the books, and to say some other writers whose names we do not know invented the character.

Let us look carefully and fairly at this view of the subject. If it be reasonable it may be true; if it be true we need not fear to accept it. Nothing in Jesus calls on men to profess to believe what to them is not the truth; nothing can be more unlike him than to use words without convictions. We cannot do otherwise than "hold fast that which is true" to us; indeed we cannot hold fast to anything else, though it be called truth by never so many voices of men.

The theory that Jesus is an invention is another way of saying that he is the hero of a romance, a creation of constructive imagination. It involves this: four Jews at about the same time, among a people not given to making books of any kind—least of all books of the imagination—were seized with desire to write books, and thus it came about that they have given to the world, as the product of dramatic genius, this character of Jesus. As, for illustration, it may be said, in a sense, that Bulwer invented the "Margrave" of *A Strange Story.*

Let us inquire into the antecedent probabilities that these men would naturally attempt to construct and put into form such a work of the imagination; nay, more: whether they were likely to attempt any dramatic work at all.

We are not left to guesses in considering such questions. It is historically certain that the Hebrew mind in ancient days was not given to this sort of literary work. The Greek mind gave dramas to the world, matchless of their kind; the Hebrew mind gave none. There is nothing in Hebrew literature of the period assigned to Jesus, of the period succeeding him, or from the time of Moses, to indicate so much as a tendency to such creations of the imagination.

We have much to judge by, and there can be no mistake. We have the Old Testament Scriptures, the apocryphal books, the comments of the scribes—called Targums—upon their sacred writing, the little book called "Acts of the Apostles," the other New Testament writings, and the works of Josephus as specimens, showing the trend and method of Hebrew literature.

The Hebrew mind in ancient days was not given to art, but to morals. The Jew did not develop art impulses till he had become cosmopolitan and Christianity had changed the world. In ancient Hebrew literature, whether in plain prose—in history, statute laws, or proverbs; whether in psalms or other poetry; whether in the magnificent imagery of the prophets, we find that morals, not art, inspire the thought and form the expression. There are neither paintings, nor statues, nor dramas. Their architecture was borrowed from the Phenicians; they were original in their ideas of morals and in their laws and customs relating to rights and wrongs. Their literature is dominated by religion, and not by art, in any of its manifold developments.

Read it all—all ancient Hebrew literature; we have history, laws, proverbs, poetry, prophecies, but we have no dramas.

You may cite me to the book of Job. This is more like a drama than any other. If this be allowed, it is the one exception. But it belongs to a period very remote from that of the evangelists, and if it be a drama it is, as may be shown, such a work as a Hebrew might have written. But the story of Jesus is not such a drama as a Hebrew of his period might have written, allowing, what is not true, that at some other period it might have been imagined by a Hebrew, or any other writer of books. As to the book of Job, it is in harmony with Hebrew characteristics and with the time and country in which its scenes are laid. The books of the evangelists are not in harmony with them; they contradict them all and utterly.

Consider well the four little books of the evangelists that we call gospels; study them just as you would any other ancient writings. See what is in them, that you may know what manner of men they were who wrote them. Reject them all, if there be reason, but look carefully to this one thing—whether these writers were given to dramatic creations, or, indeed, had faculty for such work. There is evidence enough in their writings that Matthew, Mark, Luke, and John were not of the literary and book-making classes. They were of the common people; unlearned and unskilled in literature, laboring and business men, trained as laymen. Their lives were very far removed from the occupations and influences that dominated the very feeble literary instinct that belonged to that period of Hebrew literature.

I conclude that it was antecedently as improbable that the evangelists would have attempted the production of any drama whatever, as I will show that it was impossible, had they made the attempt, for them to have invented such a story as they tell us of "The Man of Galilee."

2

"NO DRAMATIST CAN DRAW TALLER MEN THAN HIMSELF"

The doctrine I set forward concerning Jesus is this: Such a person must have actually lived, as the condition of conceiving such a character, for the reason that the power of creating such a character was never in the Hebrew mind, or any other.

At this point let me tell you how my thoughts were directed in the lines the argument takes in this discussion.

In the month of April, 1861, while a pastor in Sparta, Ga., I was reading one of Hugh Miller's books, First Impressions of England and Its People. The writer of this to me entertaining and instructive volume was comparing, on the occasion of a visit to the grave of Shakespeare, the great poet, Sir Walter Scott and Charles Dickens. Hugh Miller said (I believe the quotation is substantially correct; I have not seen the book in a long time—it was loaned to some of you): "No dramatist, whatever he may attempt, can draw taller men than himself."

I closed the book and said to myself: "Then Matthew, Mark, Luke, and John did not invent Jesus."

It was not till February, 1864, that the thought, which I often brooded, was brought into a discussion. While in camp as a missionary chaplain with Longstreet's corps of the Army of Virginia, near Greenville, East Tennessee, I sketched rudely enough, one snowy day, the outlines of an argument, using it one night, soon after, in a sermon preached in the First Methodist Church, Atlanta, Ga. In the course of years it grew upon me into a series of lectures delivered to senior classes in Emory College. It outgrew the limits of a sermon at Monticello, Ga., August, 1878. My old students and certain life-long friends will pardon this much of personal reminiscence. For reasons connected with them these personal statements are introduced.

"No dramatist can draw taller men than himself." Hugh Miller did not mean that a writer may not describe greater men than himself, but that he cannot invent a character greater than his own. It is as plain as the axiom in physics that water cannot rise above its level. That which is created cannot be greater than that which creates.

It is very common for us to write of "taller men" than ourselves; we all do this. When you were but a college-boy you did not, as you will remember, shrink from writing essays upon Cromwell, Washington, Gladstone, Bismarck, and the few such men who have lived. I have known a young man to write fairly well of even Socrates. But he had the cyclopedias. He was not creating —thinking out for himself and of himself—the good and wise old sage.

Hugh Miller says, "Dickens knows his place." The gifted novelist did not attempt great characters. Shakespeare did; he was greater than any character he produced; "taller" than any man he "drew."

When you come to ask whether these four Jews, the evangelists, could have invented the character we know as Jesus you must remember that they had, first of all, in order to do it, to throw themselves outside the sphere of Jewish thought and sentiment. If to them had been granted all personal qualifications the conditions under which they lived made the invention of such a character impossible; they could not breathe the intellectual, social, and moral air in which they lived and do it. For this character, the Jesus of the evangelists, is not in harmony with the essential characteristics of the Jewish race or with the dominant influences of that time; this character antagonizes these characteristics and influences at every point.

Granting—and it is admitting an intellectual miracle that staggers credulity—that these men did meet the first condition for the invention of such a character, and overcame, as no other men ever did in any nation or time, the controlling influences under which they reveal in these writings of themselves, they were capable of such an intellectual and spiritual feat as inventing drama that should give Jesus to the world.

To have achieved such a result they must have been in breadth, depth, and elevation of intellect capable of thinking out the mighty doctrines that Jesus taught. And this, we may well believe, was the least part of their task.

To me it is incredible that these four men could have thought out the teachings of Jesus. For such thinking they lacked all things that history and philosophy show to be necessary for such thinking.

Why could not Socrates and Plato, great, learned, wise, and good, to whom came more than glimpses of heavenly truths, think out what the Sermon on the Mount contains?

Socrates and Plato, if mere men could do such thinking, ought to have thought out the Sermon on the Mount; for they had every gift that nature could bestow and every opportunity cultured Athens could offer. And they did their best to think out the truths that bind man and God together. They failed; and Plato sighed for the coming of a divine man who would make clear what to him was dark.

If Jesus never lived then the four evangelists, or men like them, thought out his wonderful doctrines. It is unthinkable.

But theirs was a far harder task than thinking out the truths attributed to Jesus in the gospels; they had also to think out a man who lived up to them. It is easier to write a great speech than to set before the reader a man he knows to be capable of making it; but this is easier than to proclaim a lofty doctrine of morals and show a man as living up to it. Their problem, if they thought it all out, was immeasurably more than the invention of the Sermon on the Mount and of the other discourses that move so easily on the same high plane of thought and spiritual life; it was to invent a life and reveal a life in absolute harmony with these matchless discourses. But Jesus lived the Sermon on the Mount and all else that he ever taught. Not once, in the least particular, in word or deed, does he fail; always he lives up to his teaching; he incarnated his doctrine. No other human being, before or since Jesus, ever lived up to the Sermon on the Mount; the best men and women have only approximated it; and it is the best who have most realized their failure. But Jesus lived his teachings so perfectly that it is only in his life that we truly read their meaning.

How shall we measure the capacity of these four, Matthew, Mark, Luke, and John, for creating this character of Jesus? By the revelations they make in their writings of themselves: their capacity and character.

3

MATTHEW, MARK, LUKE, AND JOHN NEITHER GOOD NOR GREAT ENOUGH

How little the evangelists were capable of inventing such a character as the Jesus of the four gospels is made very plain by comparing Jesus and his doctrines with them and their notions.

It must be assumed here that you have, to some extent at least, considered what the character of Jesus is and what his teachings mean. As to your conception of him and his teachings, this I am sure of: if you continue to study him and his words your best ideas now will, by and by, seem to you to be very unworthy.

Measure the evangelists and their thoughts by Jesus and his thoughts. How small, narrow, meager, and lean of soul they are! When they speak, when they act in these histories, they give us the gauge and the level of very common men. They misapprehend him till he is rent with grief at their dullness and hardness of heart. They misinterpret his simplest words. They show in many words what even to us seems to be amazing spiritual stupidity and spiritual incapacity.

This is a fair specimen of them and their thinking powers: Jesus said to them one day, "Beware of the leaven of the Pharisees and of the Sadducees." "And they reasoned among themselves, saying, It is because we have taken no bread," supposing that he meant they must not eat bread with these people.

This also gives us the drift and gauge of their thoughts: Jesus was constantly and in many ways speaking to them of the "kingdom of heaven," and they kept dreaming and talking of a "kingdom of Israel," the restoration of David's throne. This was the common thought and talk of their circle. One of the best of the women who followed Jesus and loved him, braving danger and contempt for his sake, Salome, preferred ambitious requests for her two sons, James and John, who were in their mother's secret and sympathy, seeking high places for them in what they so longed for—the common dispensation of national deliverance and dominion.

So far below his thoughts are their thoughts, so unlike him are they, that no Christian child, who has but partially learned of Jesus what he means by the "kingdom of God," can read what Salome and her sons say to Jesus without recoiling from them.

Were the evangelists good enough—did they have the moral elevation necessary to the conception of such truths as Jesus taught? Of such a life as Jesus lived? Of Jesus himself?

If you know what is in these gospels it is too plain to you to need argument that these men were very far below the sphere of Jesus as to morals, rights and wrongs, and whatever relates to spiritual life. While he was proclaiming self-renunciation as the condition precedent to entering into life at all in common with his life, these men, while claiming to be his disciples and best friends, were wont to "dispute" with one another about seats of honor at dinings, as well as places of honor in the earthly kingdom they were looking for.

Some of them showed that they could fight upon occasion—their Galilean blood was equal to that; but they greatly lacked moral courage. They were afraid not only of men's anger, but of their criticism. But it is impossible to think of Jesus as hesitating, for one instant, from any sort of fear of men, fear of death or criticism, in uttering one truth or doing one right thing. We cannot think of Jesus as feeling the pulse of public sentiment in order to determine what he should say. We cannot think of Jesus as, for one instant, looking about him to read in the faces of his hearers, whether they were Galilean peasants or the chief estates of

Jerusalem, the probable reception of his words. We cannot think of him as veering the thickness of a line from the perfect truth as he saw it in order to win favor or avoid resentment. It is certain to us that such thoughts were never in his mind—that such feelings were never in his heart. His "eye was single," his "whole body full of light."

Do these men whose names go with the four gospels show right feeling, sentiment, for inventing such a character, granting, what we know they did not have, all other qualifications? Seeing what they were, what they show themselves to have been, is it possible to believe that, in their inmost souls, they were in sympathy with the character they have given us in the gospels? To invent a truly great, all-around character, there must be not only adequate gifts of intellect and force of conscience; there must be also right sensibility. There must not only be a large mind and a true conscience; there must be a good heart. The evangelists were not bad men, but they were unspiritual. If one cannot, as an original conception of the intellect, "draw a taller man than himself," much less can he draw a better man than himself.

Test their capacity for such a work as inventing the Jesus of the gospels in any direction. Compare these men with Jesus as to his doctrine and practice as to toleration and human brotherhood. They shrink into nothingness.

Jesus goes to the house of the publican, Zaccheus, whom all Jericho hated. Jesus dines with the man who was unpopular, who was despised; he preaches the full Gospel to him; he is kind to him; he loves him. The disciples were in sympathy not with Jesus, but the crowd that "murmured." They were mortified, displeased, afraid, scandalized; Jesus had done so imprudent a thing as to dine with a man who had no friends, but many foes.

You know of Jesus from his words, above all from his life, that he was incapable of prejudice; that no wretched or mean man of any class or race could appeal to him in vain. You know that Jesus was as free from all intolerance, from all caste feeling and race prejudice, as the virgin snow is free from stain. But his disciples, these men who have told us of him, were saturated and poisoned with these feelings; they lived on the low plane of their race and time, and not above it. In the "Acts of the Apostles" we see what that plane was; the Jew hated Gentiles. Consider the history of Peter's visit to Cornelius, and you will see how deep and inveterate is the feeling that opened a gulf between the Jews and other races. Consider what is meant by the sudden outburst of rage at the word "Gentile" that day Paul spoke to the mob in the temple court, as he stood on the castle stairs. All history illustrates this intense race prejudice. In this country, in the spring of 1888, a Jew celebrated the funeral of his daughter because she had married a Gentile.

Read the story of the Syrophenician woman, the parable of the good Samaritan, his heavenly doctrines about loving our enemies, and then think of these writers inventing Jesus and his doctrines.

See the false shame on their faces when they find Jesus talking with the woman of Sychar by Jacob's well, and ask whether men like these lived in the same world with him!

Consider the attitude of Jesus toward fallen women. See how he bore himself with the woman who washed his feet with her tears in Simon's house; see his tender respect for Magdalene; see him, his cheeks aflame with shame and confusion, his eyes dewy with pity, as he made marks on the ground with his finger that day they brought a sinful girl to him and demanded judgment upon her.

These men who wrote of Jesus were as incapable of such sentiments and conduct as they were incapable of building worlds. God pity us! as incapable as we, his disciples of today, are, who, after all that he has taught us and done for us, in our meanness and cowardice abide still in heathenism, and scorn those whom Jesus did not scorn. We may judge these evangelists by ourselves; they were as we are. They were ashamed of him when he spoke respectfully and kindly to fallen women; we would be ashamed of him now if he were again among us in the flesh, bearing himself toward our outcasts as he did when he was in Galilee.

If possible, these evangelists were as incapable as we are of inventing the character of Jesus.

In what has been said of the ability of these men to conceive such a character as Jesus remember we are not speaking of copyists, but creators; not of those who merely put together a story from materials furnished by history, or from some like that has been lived, but of those who invent, think out a character. The copyists, the historians, the biographers, the novelists, easily enough write and talk of greater and better men than themselves. This sort of literary work, this sort of thinking, is done every day; it is common as the "making of books." If the materials are furnished us we may well enough write of those who are beyond and above us. We will naturally and often necessarily do this in describing one who actually lived. Great and good men and women have often had biographers immeasurably inferior to them. A clever literary man may draw a fair picture of Julius Caesar. Froude did it. A man of hard and narrow spirit may so write of heroes as to make us feel their superiority. Carlyle did this for not a few. A small man may tell us of his master. Even Boswell could do this.

But in considering whether these four writers could have invented the character of Jesus we are not speaking of the sort of work historians and biographers do, but of pure creative work; the thinking out of a character never described by another and that never lived. For the theory we are now considering is that Jesus never lived; that he is only the product of the dramatic genius of these four writers, Matthew, Mark, Luke, and John.

Now, you will conclude when you have considered it, that very little, if any, of this sort of work is ever done. Perhaps we should hesitate to affirm that such creative work is impossible, but it may well be doubted whether any character in any fiction or drama of any sort, by any writer in any age, is a pure invention. Is there not for every character in fiction as well as in history a man somewhere, in some form? some facts in actual life that furnish the materials for the conception and delineation of that form of life that the writing presents to us? Is there in any writing any character that has not intellectual descent from some life actually lived, or in some way other than by creative processes brought into the writer's thoughts?

Consider Shakespeare's plays. Life furnished the materials; his heroes and heroines have real men and women back of them. Take

Milton's Satan. He is very like Milton in force and sublimity; but the poet did not create the character. His Satan is a composite work from Bible hints and heathen mythology. This Satan had lived in the thoughts of men before that Milton took him in hand.

Only think how difficult, if not impossible, it must be to think out a perfectly new type of character, a type that has nothing in life to stand for it. It would be like trying to conceive a sixth sense. Back of legends the noblest and the ignoblest there is some form of life or some form of fact. It may be that all ideas even not revealed have their type or origin somewhere in nature or in life. Whether with hand or brain man works upon materials furnished him; man creates nothing; man is created.

But there was in no nation whatever—and these four men knew the Jewish nation only with any fullness of knowledge—any character, any life, any facts, that could have so much as suggested Jesus. They were shut up to Hebrew history, and that could furnish no materials to the evangelists for the construction of such a character. It was not suggested by the Hebrew prophets; for it is evident that the disciples did not understand these prophecies as pointing to Jesus till after he had lived his life, till his mission was ended. Nay, with all the backward-shining light of his life no four men in the world today could, without the actual story, construct the character and life of Jesus out of what the prophets say.

There has been a good deal of fanciful writing concerning certain characters in the Old Testament history, considered as types of the Messiah. Joseph, Moses, Joshua, David—even magnificent and profligate Solomon and the coarse, dull Samson have been set forth as types of the true Son of man. Adam himself has been discussed and portrayed in this connection. Some of these men were among the greatest and best of the human race. But whatever they were as types of the Teacher, Prince, and Saviour foretold by the prophets, there was nothing in these men that could have suggested the invention of the Christ of the evangelists.

So far as the predictions in Hebrew prophecy may be urged as accounting for the conception of Jesus by the evangelists, they not only did not understand them so as to make such use of them, they misunderstood them, and, in common with their people, supposed that they foretold another and altogether different character than that of the Jesus of the gospels. Jesus had to live and die before they could understand the prophets as referring to him; it was he who unlocked their meaning. The whole Christ is not in the prophets—could not be; words could not manifest him; he had to live to be known.

Non-Christian Hebrews are to this day looking for a different character to appear and fulfill the prophets. The "Jews' Wailing Place" in Jerusalem tells travelers of our time how they cling to an interpretation of the prophets that excludes the lowly Nazarene, of whom the evangelists have told us.

4

IS JESUS AN IDEAL JEW
OF THE TIME OF TIBERIUS?

We will consider the notion that Jesus is the product of dramatic genius from other stand-points. Have the evangelists given form and voice to national ideals?

Jesus cannot be in those writings the crystallization of national legends; there are no such legends. Had these writers constructed the character out of national legends or national hopes Jesus would have been a national deliverer, not a personal Saviour, talking to men of sin and salvation. He was not at all, as these writings and as other Hebrew writings make plain, the nation's ideal of a hero and deliverer. Jesus was any thing but such an ideal; he utterly spoiled the national ideal of the Shiloh who was to come; he disappointed every expectation that rose to greet him.

Once, when the people and the priests thought they might use him as a national leader, they tried to force a king's crown upon his head. He refused their crown, and they crucified him.

There is another fatal objection to the notion that Jesus is only the invention of four romance writers, suddenly springing up among a people who did not write romances. If they invented him we should have four Christs, not one.

There are differences enough in their statements that we cannot explain in any honest way, but that would, I suppose, cease to be differences if only we knew all the facts to show that these writers were not in collusion to tell a story that would hold together. We do not know all the facts; St. John, you will remember, tells us that many things are not recorded; perhaps we have only the smaller part of them.

These four men are not alike; no two men are. They differ in style and, therefore, in temperament, gifts, training, and character. They are as different as any four writers you know; for illustration, as Carlyle, Emerson, Macaulay, and Irving differ.

To make plainer the thought I wish you to consider, take Satan as a character in literature. Compare the Satans of Milton, Goethe, Bailey, Browning, and Byron. These writers show us five, not one chief of devils. They are as unlike as their authors; and they are like their authors.

Only a woman could have drawn the Satan of Mrs. Browning. Milton's Satan is a copy of the Miltonic intellect and character—grand, scholarly, metaphysical, austere; Puritan is the hero of the Paradise Lost. Bailey's Satan grew in the atmosphere of Temple Court, and is a London lawyer of the first order with a diabolical nature. Byron's is like Byron—brilliant, moody, desperate, and vain. Goethe's is German, and brought up in Weimar. He is like the high-priest and poet of materialism who gave us Faust; like Goethe, university bred, learned, scientific, literary, all-accomplished, gay and cynical by turns, a man of the world, gentlemanly even in diabolisms, one familiar with the best society, cosmopolitan in his tastes, and nineteenth century in dress and manners as well as in his opinions and habits.

But these four men who wrote of Jesus, these men so different in their training and manner of life—Matthew, who had been a tax-collector under the Roman Government; Mark, a mere child when Jesus was among men, and brought up under a careful mother; Luke, a "physician beloved;" and John, a fisherman of Galilee—these have given us one Jesus, not four. The differences are such as four photographs of one man show in different postures taken by the same artist in the same day. No matter by whose pen recorded, the words and deeds of Jesus in the four gospels are the words and deeds of one man.

But there is another view of the notion that the evangelists invented the character of Jesus.

Granting that these men had the mental and spiritual capacity to have created such a character as that of Jesus; granting that, by some strange chance, although without precedent or succession, and in utter contradiction of all we know of the laws of the human mind, these writers, in themselves and their circumstances so different, invented not four, but one character, there is another thing to be considered, and it alone is conclusive: they were bound to have invented a different Jesus from the Jesus of the gospels.

It is impossible but that these men were under the influences that not only characterized their times but made them what they were. The gospels themselves show that these men were not only thoroughly Hebrew in their thoughts and dispositions, but Hebrews of that period. No writer can any more escape the intellectual and moral atmosphere of his time than he can escape the heredity that is in his blood. These influences will show themselves in any work of the imagination as certainly as children will resemble their ancestors.

Now Jesus, though a Jew, is not like his time or people. He is a Jew only in blood; he is not a Jew in thought or character.

The Jew of that period, saying nothing of what was past or of what was to come to that most wonderful people, was narrow in his sympathies; Jesus was as broad as humanity. The Jew was exclusive; Jesus made welcome all who came to him. The Jew had small toleration for opinions that were not his own, and none for men of other races; no cosmopolitanism, or even Christian charity, has ever yet reached the divine tolerance of Jesus. The Jew felt only contempt for the mongrel tribes of Samaria; Jesus makes a Samaritan teach us universal brotherhood. The Jew felt that contact with other nations defiled him; there is not in Jesus the faintest flavor of any sort of race or caste prejudice.

The master passion that dominated Jewish life in the days of Jesus was a fierce patriotism that expended its fires in bitter and undying hatred of Rome; Jesus, while loving his people and weeping over their impending calamities, said, "Love your enemies." If these writers were inventing a character when they wrote the gospels their hero would have been in sympathy with his time and people. Such a Christ would have unfurled the lion-ensign of Judah, and every sword would have leaped from borders of Edom. But Jesus paid tribute to Caesar and commanded his disciples to do it.

Of Jesus we may well say what he said of himself: he is "The Son of man." He belongs to all; he is a universal character, and the only one in history. He is brother to every human being; he loves one as well as another and each one perfectly. He means as much to us of today as to those friends in Bethany whom he loved, or as he meant to that "beloved disciple" who leaned upon his breast at the Last Supper.

The necessary conclusion is, such a character could not have been created by dramatic genius, least of all by the four writers of that period who have given us the gospels. The Jesus of the gospels must have lived, to have been conceived or described.

This conclusion agrees with the method these writers adopt in presenting this character to us. It is the method of perfect simplicity. They nowhere try to tell us what he was or what he was like. There are no comparisons, no analyses of qualities, no character-sketching; there is no effort, not the least, to draw a portrait of him. They simply write down what they saw him do and what they heard him say; and they make it plain that they understood neither his deeds nor his words, and that least of all they understood him.

The loftiest genius could not have invented the character of Jesus. Plain men, like Matthew, Mark, Luke, and John, could write of a life that was lived; they could write down the words they heard him speak; they could record the story of the good works they saw him do, and so make us to know Jesus, "who and what manner of man he was."

5

JESUS AND MYTHS

Some learned men, in seeking a way to account for the Jesus of the New Testament without accepting the reality of his existence, have sought to set up a notion like this: It is true that the evangelists did not invent this character, yet Jesus never really lived; he is only the myth of Hebrew history.

We are to think of Jesus, they tell us, as we do of the Greek Theseus, of the Egyptian Isis and Osiris, of the Thor and Odin of the Scandinavian legends, of the Hindustanee Vishnu, or of Buddha, and of scores of other myths that belong to the poetry, traditions, superstitions, and religions of other nations. Much scholarship has been mustered into the service of this notion. All this may appear more absurd than serious to one whose education has made Jesus of Nazareth real to his thoughts. It may indeed be so; but we must be fair even to those who seem to us to advance absurd views. I cannot doubt that some able and sincere minds have accepted a theory of Jesus that makes him out only a Hebrew myth.

Let us look at this history in a common-sense way, without burdening these pages with tiresome and confusing quotations. There are some things which may be plain enough to those who are unlearned in the writings and legends referred to—some things that the learned cannot deny. Myths are growths, and whatever grows—whether a tree, a man, a thought, or a legend—grows under certain laws that cannot be violated. There may be some laws under which myths develop unknown to me. But some of these laws are unmistakable. I mention them, and you will see for yourself that none of them are observed in the story of Jesus. The story we find in the evangelists violates them all. If the conceptions among other nations that are called myths are myths then Jesus cannot be counted among them.

1. Myths originate and, as conceptions, are complete before written history. In all nations the earliest historians relate mythological stories that antedate all letters and all records. In some nations a fragmentary history went to a sort of record before there was a true written language. Rude pictures engraved on stone or painted, and what are called cuneiform characters, such as are found on the bricks or clay cylinders among the ruins of Ninevah and Babylon, and such hieroglyphics as are found on ancient tombs in Egypt, in Mexico, and other countries—these tell us of national myths that belonged to a period ages before even these crude attempts at writing were made. The principle—it is invariable as a law—holds good in every nation that has a myth or written history of any sort.

But the Jesus of the evangelists appeared, and the story of his life was written, long after the most eventful and important history of the Hebrew race was recorded.

2. About all myths there is something grotesque if not monstrous. They are exaggerations of men or animals. Sometimes they are natural forces represented as becoming incarnate in some fantastic shape. If in human form the mythical characters are gigantic, strange, verging upon the unnatural and impossible. But Jesus appears as a man, simply; he has not a personal peculiarity to set him apart from his neighbors and companions. Not a word in the story suggests any thing abnormal or even singular. There is not a word to tell us of his personal appearance; there is no suggestion of any thing un-human or extra-human in his form or manner as he appeared among men. The halo about his head you see in pictures is the pretty conceit of the painters; there is not a hint of this, or any thing like it, in the story of the evangelists. There

is not so much as a word concerning his complexion, his stature, the color of his hair or eyes, or the tones of his voice. He is just a man among men—one who might have walked unnoticed in the streets of Jerusalem.

Read what the old books tell you of Grecian, Roman, Egyptian, and other myths. How strange they are, how different from men! Jesus appears as a man, and the evangelists have not one word to indicate that he was peculiar in appearance in any respect.

3. Myths reflect their time, place, and race. This statement is without exception. Theseus is of ancient Greece and is Greek in every sinew and lineament. Odin and Thor come to us out of the dark German forests, and are but exaggerations, in their virtues and vices, of the mighty barbarians who dwelt in them. Isis and Osiris are as like Egypt as the desert, the Nile, and its mysterious sources. Bel-Merodach is as like Chaldea as the valley of the Euphrates and its lost civilization could make him. Vishnu is as Hindustanee as the Ganges and its terrible jungles and the fierce beasts that made men afraid. And so of them every one, from the loftiest and noblest conceptions of god-like men that ever inspired the Greek imagination with great ideals down to the meanest and most devilish that ever filled the superstitions of African or Australian bushmen with terrors. But in Jesus there is not a trace of coloring from any scene or period in Hebrew history, from Abraham in Ur of the Chaldees to the days of Caesar Augustus.

4. In all nations myths defy chronology; they are without dates. In the imagination of their people they seem to have existed not only from the beginnings of national life, but to have gone before it. Think of any of them—those that have come down to us from ancient nations, as well as those that still hold their place in the folk-lore of barbarous peoples. They are all without dates. We do not read of Isis and Osiris appearing in the capital of Egypt in the days of Rameses II; the Egyptian gods are older than any of their dynasties and lived before men kept genealogies. And so of all the gods of mythology; they are without contemporaries known to any history. Myths precede the invention of calendars; if time was

counted at all the years were without dates. How utterly different is the story of Jesus, that some men tell us only a Hebrew myth!

Of Jesus and the time of his appearing it is written:

> "And it came to pass in those days, that there went out a decree from Caesar Augustus, that all the world should be taxed. And this taxing was first made when Cyrenius was governor of Syria."

Augustus was emperor; Cyrenius was governor in Syria; Herod was king in Judea.

5. Myths defy topography as they do chronology; they are not only without dates, they are without definite localities. They appeared not only some when that cannot be fixed in time, but somewhere that cannot be fixed in time, but somewhere that cannot be found as a place. Their origin is shrouded in mystery. Some of the contemporaries of Jesus made it a point against him, "As to this man we know whence he is."

In the story of Jesus we are told of places with such exactness that the statements of the evangelists are to this day the best guides to the scholarly men who make explorations in order to find relics and fragments of lost history in Palestine. They do not tell us of Jesus as appearing somewhere in their country, as Galilee, Samaria, Judea. They tell us of Nazareth, Bethlehem, Bethsaida, Capernaum, Bethphage, Bethany, the Mount of Olives. They tell us of the "beautiful gate of the temple" which, he and his disciples looked upon, and of "Jacob's well" "near to the parcel of ground that Jacob gave to his son Joseph"—the very spot where Jesus sat to rest, while his disciples went to Sychar to buy bread of the baker—the well from which a woman of the Samaritans drew water and gave him to drink.

6. Myths are not completed at once. They require a long time—ages—for their development. But the conception of the character of Jesus comes into the thought of men with his manifestation and abides through the centuries that have followed as it was first given to the world.

There is absolutely nothing like it in all Hebrew history that went before him, as there is nothing like it in the history that comes after him. And the conception of Jesus that is given by the brief accounts of the evangelists is so finished, so complete, that the attempts of after times to add to it in the stories of the so-called apocryphal gospels have utterly failed of their design. No marvelous stories, handed down from one generation to another, have in the least added to or taken from the Jesus of the evangelists. What Jesus signified when the gospels were written he has been through the centuries that have followed him. What he was then he is today.

7. All myths belong to the infancy, never to the age of any nation. They spring out of the morning mists; they never appear in the light of day. If the story of Jesus had been placed in Chaldea, before the call of Abraham, it also would have belonged to the infancy of a race. To harmonize with the laws that govern the development of myths the story of Jesus should have anticipated the first chapters of Hebrew history; it should have been placed in that uncertain period that includes the dispersion from Armenia, the second cradle of the human race.

But the story of Jesus is given to the world, fresh and complete, with not one hint of it in all preceding history, in the last years, the closing days of Hebrew national life in Judea.

The story antedates but a little while the destruction of Jerusalem by Vespasian and his Roman legions; when Jesus was born Augustus was emperor; when Jesus entered upon his ministry Tiberius Caesar was in the fifteenth year of his reign; his lieutenant, Pontius Pilate, governed Judea as a subject province, and his soldiers kept the peace in the holy city.

Consider how impossible it is for myths to originate after written history, in the sun-glare of life in a full-grown nation. Even the pretty stories of King Arthur and his Knights of the Round Table belong to that far-away period in England when there was no written history worth the name, when letters were almost unknown, when all was young and fresh and ignorant and the fairies still ruled in the forests.

Think of a myth starting up today in London under the shadow of St. Paul's and Parliament House. Think of the world in our time talking of "Chinese Gordon" if there had lived no "Chinese Gordon." If the people who have letters, and write histories, and "turn the world upside-down" with the gospel story, should leave the poor savages of the Congo Valley to themselves, thousands of years from our times Livingstone and Stanley will live in African traditions as godlike men; and so new myths will be born, will grow and fix themselves in the legends of these lands where they have done many wonderful works—but London and New York will breed no myths concerning Livingstone and Stanley.

6

JESUS AND HEBREW HUMAN NATURE

There are writers who see clearly that the four evangelists could not have invented the character of Jesus, and who know that the story of his manifestation violates every known law that governs the birth and growth of myths; but they tell us Jesus was nevertheless only a man. They say he did really live in Palestine in the days of Augustus, Tiberius, Herod, and Pilate, and that he was only a man after all—a man of very great gifts and virtues, the best man and the greatest teacher that ever lived. This means that human nature was capable of producing Jesus; it means that Hebrew human nature in that country and in that age was capable of producing Jesus, his doctrines and his life. In other words, he was a most extraordinary but still a natural product of his race, country, and time; the normal product, though the consummate flower, of Jewish life.

In considering that the evangelists, granting them ability of all sorts for the invention of so perfect a character and such a character, must have given us a different character, some of the difficulties of the natural development theory were incidentally brought into view. But there are other matters to be fairly considered in connection with this method of accounting for Jesus.

Jesus, in one of the simplest—yet it is one of the profoundest and most comprehensive of philosophical principles—gave us the germ of our inductive philosophy and our modern scientific method. When he said, "By their fruits ye shall know them," he taught us that we are to make our theories conform to ascertained facts rather than explain our facts by our preconceived theories. It is by the fruit we are to know what the quality of the tree is.

What manner of fruit grew on this long-lived Hebrew tree? You can seek the answer for yourself; all Hebrew history will tell you.

Begin with the story of Abraham, in Genesis, and follow through the centuries the thread of Hebrew history to the times of Caesar Augustus and of Jesus, if you will, till our own time. We find in that history patriarchs, law-givers, priests, judges, soldiers, kings, statesmen, poets, reformers, and prophets. We have Abraham and the other patriarchs; Moses, Aaron, and his successors; Joshua and his compatriots; Samuel, last and best of a long line of judges; Saul, David—poet, as well as soldier and king; Solomon, genius and philosopher, sage and profligate; Isaiah and the other prophets; Nehemiah and other reformers; Daniel, the statesman, in the service of an alien prince, the conqueror of his people. In later times we have Judas Maccabaeus, the heroic defender of his country, and the other mighty men who gave their lives in a hopeless struggle for the freedom of their nation. Still later we read of men like Annas and Caiaphas, the wicked high-priests of an evil time. We have Gamaliel, learned in the law, and his pupil, Saul of Tarsus. (But for Jesus there would have been no Paul.) We have the men brought to view as "disciples" of Jesus. Later on appear such a man as Josephus and the brave men who fought the Romans and died for Jerusalem. Consider them all, the strong and the weak, the good and the bad, as they grew upon this Hebrew tree. These men show the best as well as the worst it could do. We must judge this tree by its fruits.

Can we place Jesus among them and count him as one of them—the best of them? Could a tree which produces these others produce him? To ask the question is to answer it.

I know what some writers have to say when they speak of finding types of Jesus among those who lived before him; what they say of Moses, Joshua, and others. Some of them were truly great and good men—among the best the human race can show for itself. But we cannot place Jesus among them; they do not approach him, and they are not like him. He stands alone and apart. He is not only above them, he is unlike them. The question is not simply whether the Hebrew tree, judging it by all its other fruits, was capable of producing this one perfect character in all the world, but also whether it could have produced this kind of character? Certainly it never did before him or after him. Search history for one shadow of proof that this race—wonderful and unique in all times and countries—from Abraham to Disraeli had in it any powers that could, as a normal development, produce Jesus of Nazareth.

If you will you may give your inquiries wider range. Forget that Jesus was a Jew by blood and birth and training. Try all history; search the records of other nations. Tell me of the sages and reformers—the great and good men of other people and countries; of Zoroaster, Confucius, Socrates, Buddha, and the rest; of Moses or any other Jew you could name along with them. Is Jesus only one of them? The best of them perhaps—but only one of them? Read all you may of them as their best friends tell their stories, and you would recoil if some maker of cyclopedias should talk of only adding the name of Jesus.

It is not simply that you have heard your mother pray to Jesus; it is not simply the prompting of your "cradle faith." The reason lies deeper; if today for the first time you were to read of the great and holy men of other nations and of Jesus you must think of him, without waiting to reason why, in a place by himself, as a great star shines alone. No light is so splendid but the eye knows the sunlight for what it is.

But it is not, as you know, a question as to what the human race in some age could do; it is, what could the Hebrew race do in the age of Caesar Augustus? For Jesus was of the Hebrew race and of that age.

But for the moment forget this limitation of our inquiry and ask, What could that age do? It is like asking, What could the Roman race and civilization do? For the glory of Egypt and Babylon had long departed, and the great Greeks were before the time of Jesus. Roman life then dominated the world, and Roman life did its utmost in producing Julius Caesar. But there was not in Roman life, tradition, thought, sentiment, one quality or influence of any sort whatsoever that could have any relation to the production of a character like this that the evangelists have given us.

But at last we must ask simply this question: What could the Hebrew race in that age do?

Only Jewish influences entered into the life of Jesus. There is not in any single thought or word of his so much as an echo of any thing characteristic of other peoples. There is not an undertone in his thoughts from the Greek or Roman masters. He had nothing from other teachers or thinkers. He was only a Jew, never out of Palestine, of a peasant family in Galilee. The Galilean was a narrow, suspicious, and revengeful man; provincial to the last degree; holding fast old ideas and rejecting new ones with little regard to argument or evidence—the "Bourbon" of his time. He was a man of bitterer prejudices than characterized even the men of Judea. But even Galilee had its best and its worse, and Jesus was brought up in a disreputable mountain town. "Can there any good thing come out of Nazareth?" was a common proverb, carrying its own answer and indicating the estimate placed upon the little town by the better people of the country.

Jesus was untaught in the greater schools of his own people. "How knoweth this man letters, having never learned?" implies more than that his hearers knew his history well enough to know he was not school-trained as their scribes were; it means that they knew he did not speak as their scholars spoke. Jesus did not talk like a book; he was not learned in books; his language indicates, so far as books count, knowledge of the Scriptures only; he could read, but he was no scholar.

Compare now the conditions under which this young carpenter of Nazareth, working at his trade, and doing good work till he was thirty years old, grew into manhood; consider what his people were at their best; consider how little of what was best in Hebrew life entered into his Galilean bringing up; consider the hard conditions and the narrow limitations of his life, and tell me whether Jesus is a normal development of his race and time and place?

We will now speak of his teachings; compare him with his natural conditions. There is nothing in all human history that makes it possible to believe that a mere Jew, brought up in that Nazareth, could have become this flawless, perfect character. If it be otherwise there is nothing, absolutely nothing, in heredity or environment; then any soil can produce any fruits. Better expect to find the kingly trees of the Yosemite Valley growing with the stunted sage of Arizona.

Consider the teachings of Jesus and tell me can this perfection of truth come out of Nazareth? Consider what he teaches about God, the human soul, sin, reconciliation, salvation and immortality. Consider how he teaches and illustrates in his life the brotherhood of the human race. Consider his ethics—his doctrines of rights and wrongs. What he teaches about rights and wrongs, in principle and practice, is so absolutely full and perfect that good men—the best men in the world today, so long after his time—cannot so much as conceive of one single virtue he did not teach or of one single evil that he did not condemn. Nay, the wisest and best are always trying to teach men the truth Jesus taught; and his standard is so high that no sane and honest man has ever professed to have reached it.

One writer has ventured, in order to find one spot on this sun, to say, Jesus did not teach patriotism! His whole life was devoted to his people; his doctrines nourish and conserve patriotism. He did not teach the thing a mere partisan of a clan or tribe calls patriotism; then he would have been only a Galilean zealot. He teaches the only patriotism a good man can respect—a love of country that believes in righteousness and the golden rule that loves its own and another's too. If Jesus be only a man—a Galilean Jew, we must remember—he contradicts in his flawless all-around character and perfect teaching the conditions of his life. This perfection of character and teaching on the one hand, and this Galilean Jew and Nazarene carpenter on the other, not only do not agree, they cannot exist together. It is by his life that we realize how imperfect all others are; it is by his teachings that we test the rights and wrongs of all other teachings.

There is absolutely nothing in his race or age that accounts for Jesus. That he was a normal product of his race and age contradicts every law of life we know. If it be not so all history goes for nothing and there is no law or reason in the nature of things.

7

His Method of Thought Differences Him From Men

In studying the story of the evangelists let us try to come nearer to Jesus. We need not fear; he would have us find out all about him that we can; he would have us know what manner of man he is. If we love beauty, goodness, and truth, we will approach him with reverence. No good man, no man you can respect or trust, will speak of Jesus with flippant words. But we may go to him without hesitation; he who took little children in his arms and blessed and kissed them will not receive the humblest student with coldness. Indeed, the more one needs him the more welcome he is. It was he who said to the "weary and heavy laden," "Come unto me."

Let us consider now, as best we may, what we must call his method of thought. It differences him utterly from all mere human teachers. We can find many illustrations.

In the first place, Jesus does not seek the same end that the great thinkers, who have given the world its philosophy and its science, always seek—the creation of an intellectual system of and for the universe. Humboldt, who was a very learned and gifted man, gives us a great work he calls Cosmos. It tells all he knew, or thought he knew, of the universe, and explains it all as best he could. He is one among many; all the philosophers try to account for things, and the greater they are the more they try.

In the human mind there is a resistless tendency to search into secret things, and to construct a philosophy of them. Aristotle gave us his Categories; the moderns try their hand in the same line of things. It means only this; men who are philosophers and thinkers seek to classify all facts and to find out and express— "formulate" is the word—a complete, all-embracing, all-explaining law of them.

Witty Dr. Oliver Wendell Holmes, in his Poet at the Breakfast-Table, gives us a pretty satire on this invincible disposition and always disappointed and disappointing effort of thinkers. His "Philosopher" was ever just about to find expression for his great discovery—just about to state the all-comprehensive law, the perfect formula, that left out nothing and explained it all.

It is essentially a man's way; in all departments we see the tendency and effort of men to explain the universe.

The chemist talks of "atoms" because he wishes to get down to the basis of things—to know the ultimate fact, beyond which analysis cannot go. The ontologist talks of "germs" for a like reason; he is ever striving to find a something—a substance or a force—that will explain to him not one but every life process. And the greater ones are seeking always to explain the origin of all things—to show how the universe was started or got itself going.

The philosopher who studies mind seeks the same sort of end— the construction of a mental science that embraces every fact and explains every mystery of mental action. The theologian is in the same drift; he wants a philosophy of religion. He seeks to explain God, and, in not a few instances, seems to labor more earnestly with his own nature and government than to show the sinner how to be saved. The theologian labors to show what the origin of evil is, and to make his view a philosophy that will harmonize all differences and explain all mysteries.

The strength of this tendency in mere men—and it is strongest in the greatest—to find a statement that may account for all things is shown in the absurd conclusions that some of them, entirely sane on other subjects, accept for themselves and urge upon other minds. A great chemist concludes that the universe was "once latent in a fiery cloud," and seems content with a form of pretty words. Another expounder of mysteries accounts for life in our world by telling us the "germs" were first brought from somewhere in space by "falling meteorites," pays his worship to what he dreams is science, and is content to push his problem further from him. The notion that the word "protoplasm" is supposed to stand for represents another effort to explain all things, albeit by a theory harder to understand than the universe it would embrace and expound. These are only specimens; both ancient and modern times abound in them. Wiser, perhaps, and quite as scientific was the desperation of that student of the mysteries of life and man who concluded that the "missing link" must be in the bottom of the Indian Ocean; for no diver can prove what is not in water so deep as this fathomless sea.

What we are now considering is a resistless tendency in thinking minds. It is not peculiar to one class of men; it does not characterize one age. It is simply human nature to ask questions and seek explanations. Consider a few names now mentioned and see for yourself that the greater the mere man the more he tries to explain the universe—to find a formula large enough to contain it, to classify its facts and correlate its forces. Think of these men and the few whose names should go with them—Socrates, Plato, Aristotle, Origen, Augustine, Pelagius, Athanasius, Calvin, Edwards, Leibnitz, Bacon, Humboldt, Kant, Cuvier, and, perhaps, some new men. Philosophers, scientists, theologians, they are all alike in this—they are building a system, a philosophy of the universe.

Do not mistake my purpose in these illustrations; the disposition which we have been considering is a pure human instinct; it is resistless, and it is the condition of mental activity. The mind that does not ask questions, that does not knock at the closed doors of knowledge, is stagnant and will perish. Progress and growth depend upon inquiry. Wise men will cheer every earnest student, whether he is trying to find what an atom is or what the stars contain. It is a man's way to seek to explain all things; the effort affords the drill and discipline that make growth and progress possible to the race.

But in these respects, as in so many others, Jesus is utterly un-like the philosophers and scientists and theologians. He does not in the least seek the end that mere men seek. He makes us un-derstand the universe—matter and mind, man and God—bet-ter than all of them put together. But he nowhere accounts for things. He has not a word about the "cosmos." He makes no in-quiry, raises no question, offers no explanation concerning the or-igin of things. In him there seems to be no consciousness of the mysteries of the universe, either as to its origin or nature.

But it may be said Jesus taught morals, religion, not science or philosophy, and he had no occasion to construct a system of the universe. In morals and religion, more than anywhere else, do mere men build systems when they think, explain things when they teach. But Jesus, teaching morals and religion, was unlike all others, mere men, teaching morals and religion. He said not one word—he, the only teacher who seemed to understand it—about the "origin of evil," the subject that has vexed not a little theology into lunacy; he, the only one who has seemed capable of doing it, has given us no "theodicy," nor so much as seemed to think of it at all.

He did not, he who made claim to perfect knowledge of God, explain God or philosophize about God; Jesus did not so much as give us a philosophy of himself, his life, or his mission. It was John, the disciple, not Jesus, the Master, who wrote of the Logos. Jesus offers no philosophy of the plan of salvation; he does not philosophize concerning faith, or prayer, or immortality.

As to evil, Jesus tells men what evil is, shows the ruin it brings upon them, and points out to them the way of deliverance. He talks to men of their evil and the way to make an end of it.

Jesus never investigates. He never doubts his knowledge or questions for one instant the grounds of it. We have no fit word for his method; intuition is perhaps as good as any. His thinking is not a process; it is like seeing, not learning, the truth; seeing not the outside of things as men see them, but the inside of them as God sees them.

Jesus never uses those forms of logic that are absolutely necessary to all others. We are speaking of his "method of thought;" perhaps such words do not apply to him at all. How did he find out what was true? He did not seem to find it out at all; it seemed to be in him. He never seems to discover a truth. He does not, by reasoning from what is to what must be, find out what he did not know before.

In geometry we begin with what we call "axioms," a few simple principles that need no proof. We call them "self-evident," because we see that they are true, that they must be true, the instant we know what the words mean that state them to us. Upon these we build our geometry and all the science and art that rest upon it or grow out of it. When we prove one thing we did not know by something that, being self-evident, needs no proof, we put the two together and prove a third, and so on as far as we can go. Jesus would have known the third, and the hundredth, and the last, as he knew the first—without this building-up process. He would know all that the axioms contain as we know the axioms.

For want of fitter words we have been speaking of his "method of thought." As these words have significance to mere men, Jesus, it seems, had no method of thought; he did not, as men must do, think to know; he knew things. Perhaps this is in part what he meant when he said to Pilate, "I am the Truth."

8

"NEVER MAN SPAKE LIKE THIS MAN"

We will consider the method of Jesus as a teacher, and the word is appropriate now. He did have a method in teaching men the truths that he knew without reasoning about them, the truths that he did not discover by investigation, the truths he knew because they were in him.

To begin with, Jesus does not seek to prove things to his hearers; he announces what is truth as God announces truth. He is a divine dogmatist; he offers no proof of what he sets forth as truth.

No other teacher ever taught as Jesus did. What we may call his logic-form is pre-eminently the teacher's; but no teacher ever employed it as did he who came out of Nazareth. He reasons from the weaker to the stronger reason. He does not reason to prove truth to others, as he does not reason to discover it for himself, but to teach it. This is the form of reasoning we find in all his parables and illustrations. His arguments are designed to help his learners understand what he meant and to impress it upon their minds. He never seems concerned about proving to men the truth of what he said, but only to make it plain and to enforce it. Many illustrations might be given; let a few suffice.

One day Jesus was teaching his disciples the doctrine of God's providence. He makes no argument to prove that there is a providence; he does not seek to convince them, but only to help them realize in their own thoughts the all-embracing, unfailing, and gracious providence that kept them. And he did this not to make them understand the doctrine of providence, but to help them trust in it. He seeks to bring home to them the truth he does not seek to prove. How does he set about it? What is his method? Not a mere man's method. It is indeed an absolutely simple method; but no other teacher, who has not learned it of him, has used it so in discoursing of such truths.

He begins with what they knew: "Consider the lilies of the field, how they grow; they toil not, neither do they spin; and yet I say unto you that even Solomon in all his glory was not arrayed like one of these." They knew the lilies—that is, they were used to seeing them, the little flowers so common, so insignificant, yet so beautiful. Jesus concludes: "Wherefore, if God so clothe the grass of the field, which today is, and tomorrow is cast into the oven, shall he not much more clothe you, O ye of little faith?"

In the same way he reasons of sparrows and men. He would inspire his disciples with the courage that has its root in faith in God's loving and unfailing providence. He says to them the great God not only feeds the poor little birds, but cares for them, "Are not two sparrows sold for a farthing? and one of them shall not fall on the ground without your Father. But the very hairs of your head are all numbered. Fear ye not therefore, ye are of more value than many sparrows."

He would teach his disciples the folly of forgetting what is essential in brooding anxieties about small things: "And which of you with taking thought [worrying] can add to his stature one cubit? If ye then be not able to do that thing which is least, why take ye thought for the rest?...Therefore I say unto you, Take no thought for your life, what ye shall eat; neither for the body, what ye shall put on. The life is more than meat, and the body is more than raiment."

He would make men see how perfectly simple and unmysterious is prayer and how absolutely certain it is that God will answer. Have we not listened to mere men—preachers they called themselves, yet doing, it may be, the best they could—mystifying simpleminded people and little children—themselves most of all—with tortuous disquisitions concerning the "subjective" and "objective" results of their devotions! Answering infidels, they suppose!

Jesus makes no argument about the nature of prayer; he has not a word to prove its reasonableness or to harmonize the doctrine with law. He says: "Ask, and it shall be given you; seek, and ye shall find, knock, and it shall be opened unto you. For every one that asketh, receiveth; and he that seeketh, findeth; and to him that knocketh it shall be opened."

How does he prove what he affirms? He does not prove it; he brings it home to them: "What man is there of you, whom if his son ask bread, will he give him a stone? Or, if he ask a fish, will he give him a serpent?"

Every hearer, whether parent or child, answered out of his heart, "There is not such a man among us." Jesus concludes: "If ye then, being evil, know how to give good gifts unto your children, how much more shall your Father which is in heaven give good things to them that ask him?"

The cold and cruel Pharisees, playing at religion and seeking their own, complained one day that Jesus healed a poor maimed man on the Sabbath day. Jesus made no argument about the nature of the Sabbath. He reminded them that they would lift a sheep out of the ditch on the Sabbath day, and concludes with a question that brought the truth home to them: "How much then is a man better than a sheep?"

These same people, contending about the forms of religion and forgetting God and man, complained that Jesus kept company with "publicans and sinners," and was kind to them. In answer he told them of the shepherd who, missing one sheep from his flock of a hundred, could not be content with the ninety and nine, but went out into the wilderness seeking the lost one; he told them how glad the shepherd was when in his arms he had tenderly brought it home. He told them also of the woman who could not rest till, with broom and candle, she had searched her house for the piece of money she had lost. He told them of her neighbors rejoicing with her when she had found it. Why he cared for publicans and sinners he made plain when he added: "I tell you there is joy in the presence of the angels of God over one sinner that repenteth."

Jesus would make these hard guardians of what they called the Church and despisers of their brother-men realize the Fatherhood of God. He made no argument of the sort mere men would make.

He tells them of the two sons and how glad the old father was when his poor prodigal got home. The conclusion no human heart can miss: the infinite Father, infinitely better than any earthly father, is infinitely glad when his prodigals return to him. The heart that once takes in this story of the two sons can never again tremble and cower before that horribly heathen conception of God that makes him only an infinite terror, seated on the throne of the universe, to be afraid of, fled from, and hated forever.

Jesus sought to encourage the most despondent and abject to trust in the divine justice as well as mercy. There is no lofty argument concerning the righteousness of God. He tells of the widow and the unjust judge, who feared not God nor regarded man, the judge who made a boast of heartlessness and apologized to himself for seeming to do a good deed. He grants the widow's prayer because he was selfish and mean; he would not be "wearied with her importunities." Jesus concludes: "And shall not God avenge his own darlings who cry day and night unto him?"

How clear Jesus made what mere human teachers make dark! What even some preachers of our times, too proud in their false learning to be simple in their methods and language, make so tiresome and so bewildering to hungry souls who ask for bread and get chaff!

We will not understand how unlike the methods of mere men is the method of Jesus till we have wearied ourselves with what they call reasonings; till we have come to understand that no man can teach religion who rejects the methods of Jesus for what he thinks are the methods of what he calls logic and philosophy, truly understanding neither.

What we may call his manner, as distinguished from his method of teaching, differences Jesus from mere men. No great teacher, unless it be some one who has learned of him the true secret of teaching—and how far below the Teacher the best and wisest fall!—ever before or since has the manner of Jesus.

There is a sort of fatality about men's teaching. Vanity or ignorance makes them seek to appear profound when they are only obscure. What unspeakable relief and blessing it would bring to all churches and schools if pastors and teachers would only study the method of Jesus and seek to imitate the simplicity of Jesus! Teachers, not a few of them, burden and bewilder their pupils with the dead lumber of learning that is not knowledge; preachers, not a few of them, mystify and mislead their hearers with reasonings, philosophies, and argumentations, mere war of words for the most part, that are not gospel nor life. When Jesus talked of the deepest and highest questions, of God and man, of rights and wrongs, of life and death, of time and eternity, of heaven and hell, it is said, "The common people heard him gladly." This could never be said of even the good Socrates, or the great Plato; for the "common people" could not understand them.

It is indeed a rare thing that the "common people" hear "gladly" a teacher of science, philosophy, or religion whom the uncommon people call great. As a rule, the greater one is, as men measure greatness, the less do "common people" hear him "gladly," and least of all when he speaks or writes upon the very greatest of themes. Is it because such teachers are not themselves brothers to the common people? One reason is the great men do not truly understand what they teach. And herein is a reason for patience.

Perhaps, for the most part, the great ones do the best they can. It seems that, when a mere man seeks to think profoundly or to speak strongly, he must fall into obscurity. this obscurity cannot be due to any inherent difficulty in the truth itself, but to those limitations, mental and spiritual, that belong to mere human teachers. But Jesus taught the greatest truths in language as simple and clear as when he spoke of the most familiar duties of daily life. His manner is as easy and his words as plain when speaking of immortality as when telling men to be honest and to "love one another."

Compare the Sermon on the Mount and the writings of the

greatest and best of men who have discoursed upon these themes. How perfectly simple and transparent and easy the manner and style of Jesus! How complex and dark and difficult the manner and style of men! How it should shame mere men into meek simplicity when they read of Jesus, the divine Teacher, "The common people heard him gladly!"

After all, it may be that our method of thought is as unfitted for understanding the Gospel as our method of teaching is unfitted for expounding it. It may be that if we worried ourselves less with what men have written of his words—too often trying to read into his teachings thin philosophies; if we brooded more upon his words and less upon men's notions of his words, we would understand Jesus better. Then we also could teach the people. Then, it may be, the "common people" would hear us "gladly." If we preached his "text" more and books about his "text" less we would preach more truth that saves and less philosophy that bewilders.

In speaking of the method and manner of Jesus there is another matter, not easy to discuss, that should be mentioned; I refer to the effect upon himself of his thoughts and words.

There is a divine calmness in him never seen in mere men; that is impossible to them. In this also he stands apart from men.

His greatest discourses are without intellectual heats. This is wonderful to me. He shows himself to be the tenderest-hearted teacher who ever sought to lead men out of darkness into light. We know that he is not cold of heart; we know how deep is his compassion on men; how infinite his concern for them. But he delivers the most tremendous truths with the most perfect composure and balance of spirit. If a mere man were to see clearly for the first time what the Sermon on the Mount, the third chapter of John, the parable of the Prodigal, and a score of other discourses and revelations like them really signify; if a mere man were, so to speak, to come suddenly upon such thoughts, such conceptions, so vast, deep and high, it would unbalance him. His brain would be on fire and his heart would break with holy excitement. But Jesus speaks these truths with perfect calmness; they were not new thoughts to him; there was no effort in order to grasp them or to express them. Yet Jesus was full of sympathy. He wept with the sisters at the grave of Lazarus and bewailed the fate of Jerusalem with sobs and tears.

You have read a story of Sir Isaac Newton, which, whether it be historically true or false, well illustrates, for it is very like a man, what is here brought to your attention, as showing how Jesus differs from a mere man. When Sir Isaac had nearly finished his deep and long-continued studies of the laws which govern the movement of the heavenly bodies, and was near enough the end of his great mathematical calculations to foresee the result and to realize that it would justify his sublime speculations concerning the controlling law of the material universe, he became so excited—cold philosopher and trained to self-control as he was—that he could not complete the simple processes involved in his formula. It was necessary to call in a friend to finish the easy work for him; for the moment the great astronomer was out of balance.

Sir Isaac's was exactly a mere man's way; great inventors have gone mad when they were within one step of triumph.

But Jesus was calm when speaking, in the simplest way, of the greatest truths of life and the most stupendous events that await eternity for their unfolding.

No wonder those who, on one occasion, were sent to lay hands on him had only this answer when they returned to their masters without him: "Never man spake like this man."

9

THE SON OF MAN AND SIN

When we compare the work Jesus proposed to do in the world with the schemes of earth's greatest ones we cannot classify him with mere men.

What did he think he came into the world to do? What did he consider his mission to be?

We cannot be in the least doubt for the answer; there was no confusion in his thought, no ambiguity in his words. If we ask what Jesus thought his mission was we will easily find the answer—unparalleled by the thought of any, absolutely unique, stupendous, but as unmistakable in meaning as simple in the form of expression.

We will answer in his own words: "The Son of man is come to seek and to save that which is lost." "I came not to call the righteous, but sinners to repentance." "God sent not his Son into the world to condemn the world, but that the world through him might be saved." "I came not to judge the world, but to save the world." More forcibly, if possible, than in his words, his conception of his mission is shown by his work, his living, and his dying. St. Luke, in the Acts of the Apostles, gives us in a simple statement the whole history; it is, in a line, the biography of the God-man, "He went about doing good."

That Jesus should have seen in the world evil that needed to be remedied, that he should have tried to remedy the evil he saw, does not, in itself, difference him from good and wise men who have observed the facts of human life and have deplored human miseries. All the great teachers and reformers have recognized evil in the world, and many of them have distinctly recognized this evil as moral evil. The doctrine of Jesus is peculiar in this; all the evil that is in the world is moral evil, and all moral evil is, at its root, sin, and sin, considered as a quality in man's character, is a state of being that is out of harmony with God; considered as a fact, it is life in violation of God's law. The bad man is, in his spirit, at enmity with God; in his life he breaks God's law. He loves evil because evil is in him; his life is wicked because his heart is bad.

And Jesus comes to take away sin; to deliver men from it, its penalty, and its power. Said the angel to Mary: "Thou shalt call his name Jesus, for he shall save his people from their sins."

In the view of Jesus sin is the one evil; deliverance from sin is deliverance from all evil; it is salvation. He struck at sin as the root of all possible evil; he recognized no evil that was in man's circumstances, as if his evil came out of fate or in some way invincible by him; it is all of sin.

Wherefore Jesus does not set about bettering man's circumstances, by direct effort improving the sanitary, economic, political, or social conditions of life; he works upon man himself. Whatever improves man's condition is, in the doctrine of Jesus, to be desired; but it is not enough to make man comfortable; he must be made good. He teaches that all that is truly good and needful will come to men who are delivered from sin, and that no real good can come to him whose sin remains in him. First, last, all the time, Jesus makes deliverance from sin the one thing needful—the chief good.

As his manner was, he does not argue about it; he states his doctrine positively, "with authority," as one knowing the whole truth of the case. There is no qualifying word to tone down his statements and to leave place for retreat from possible mistakes.

His doctrine he taught and illustrated in every possible way. It is in his more formal discourses, his briefest comments on men and things, his most occasional conversations and most incidental remarks. His doctrine is in all his efforts to do men good, as it is in every warning and every promise.

And there is never a shadow doubt, a suspicion of hesitation. From his first word to the last, from the beatitudes to the prayer on the cross, it is always the same thing; man's trouble is all in his sin; his only salvation is deliverance from sin.

It comes out in the most incidental way. When the penitent Magdalene washed his feet with her tears, at Simon's table, he said not a word about her lost social position or of its possible restoration. He said, "Thy sins are forgiven; thy faith hath saved thee; go in peace."

When the four kind and loving friends of Capernaum—whose names we would like to know—had brought their palsied neighbor to Peter's house, and had at last, with much trouble, through the broken roof laid him down at the feet of Jesus, the first words were not about palsy and healing, but about sin and salvation: "Son, thy sins be forgiven thee." This is what the story of the penitent publican, crying out, "God be merciful to me a sinner," means. It is what the story of the prodigal means; it is what the whole life and teaching of Jesus mean.

We must notice particularly that the mere conception of a divine incarnation is not peculiar to the story of Jesus. The notion of incarnation, the idea of the gods taking a form of flesh and manifesting themselves to men, is in the traditions of almost every nation. It has been said, hastily, I believe, that there are some races, at least some tribes, so low in development as to have no idea of God whatever. It is easy to be mistaken in such matters; it is difficult for a cultivated man to find out what a savage really thinks about any subject, least of all his religion. Perhaps the language difficulty is the least bar to understanding in such a case; the differences between men are not measured by differences in speech only. It is certain that the conception of God is, in some form, in most nations. I believe it is in all. And in every nation there is some sort of notion of divine manifestation.

The attempt to represent the gods in stone, in metal, in wood, or even in rude drawings and paintings, comes after a traditional belief has long held its place in men's thoughts of their manifestation in some visible and tangible form.

It is not always a human form; it is generally not a human form, except as it is part of the conception: as in the eagle-headed Belus of Babylon, as in the winged bulls, with the head of a man and the feet of a lion, that Layard found in the ruins of Ninevah. These composite images represented ideas of the gods, not facts concerning them. Thus the image found in the ruins of Ninevah represented strength, swiftness, courage, intelligence. But the ideas expressed in these strange and grotesque forms grew out of traditions of divine manifestation, of incarnation.

All the mythologies tell us of incarnations; but the idea of divine incarnation in the story of the evangelists differs, not in some incidents, but in all essentials from all others. One unique fact, as has heretofore, in a different connection, been pointed out, is that Jesus was simply a man who, as to his appearance, had absolutely nothing that was peculiar. Neither stature, beauty, swiftness, nor strength is attributed to Jesus.

We might speak of the limitations that go with other conceptions of gods incarnate. They are specialized by race and localized by country. This thought has been illustrated elsewhere. It may answer now simply to remind you that Vishnu is Hindustanee, Isis and Osiris Egyptian, Odin and Thor Scandinavian. Not one of them has relations to the whole human race. But Jesus, who calls himself "the Son of man," is of all, and belongs to all.

But the most notable difference to be considered now, that which alone would place Jesus apart from all others, whether men or legendary gods, is in the end he proposed to accomplish. The gods became incarnate and appeared to men, or dwelt among them, to do many and very different things; Jesus to do just one thing, and to do what no other ever proposed to do, or so much as thought of doing. He, "the Son of man," was of all and for all, and he proposes an end that concerns all. The evil he would remove from all is not a Hebrew trouble; it is in the human race.

This is plainer in comparison. Vishnu, the supreme god of Hindustanee mythology, has condescended, so the old stories tell us, to almost innumerable incarnations. But for what end? Always to work some prodigies; to do some strange things on the plane of men's lives; to do things affecting men's circumstances, not men's character. He comes to do something in a limited sphere; something for his people, Hindustanee people, not for the whole race of man. Vishnu, when he comes in mercy, comes to remedy external conditions; he delivers from pestilence, famine, wild beasts, poisonous serpents. When he comes in wrath it is to crush his enemies.

In mythology, the very conception men had of the coming of the gods grew out of their circumstances. Thus in India the conception of evil itself was determined by conditions peculiar to India. With them evil grew out of the jungles where pestilence was bred, serpents abounded, and fierce man-eating tigers hid themselves and waited for their prey. It was determined by those conditions of life peculiar to dense populations, subject to the scourges that followed was, and evil natural conditions—plague and famine.

The evil Jesus considered was peculiar to no people and to no country; it did not grow out of natural conditions; it was in man himself, and it was sin.

Among warlike nations the gods came down to take part in mere national matters; they fought the battles of their friends and punished their enemies. Your Homer tells you all this in the story of the siege of Troy. Virgil tells you the same thing; your classical authors are full of it. The poor Indians and negro tribes tell of such incarnations.

It was this very human conception of divine incarnation that filled the national imagination and sustained the national hopes before Jesus came. Such an incarnation they were longing for when they rejected him because they could not use him for their ends; it is a conception that to this day lingers in Hebrew thought and hope. They looked and prayed for a divine warrior-king who would lead their armies, restore their nation, and give it dominion over the world.

How incredible the idea that the evangelists have only given is

a reflection of popular sentiment, the outgrowth of national traditions! These sentiments and traditions were utterly spoiled by the
sort of incarnation the evangelists describe. The nation resented
unto death the conception Jesus had of his mission to men; before
such a king as Jesus they preferred the Caesar they hated; they put
to death the man who only sought to save them from their sins because he disappointed them in their patriotic ambitions.

Speaking in a general way, the gods of the nations, when they
become incarnate, come to do a man's sort of work. They work
upon the outside of life; they seek to deliver man from external
evils and to improve his external conditions. The "twelve labors
of Hercules" tell us what men thought they needed a divine man
to do; the evangelists tell us what the divine Man thought men
needed that he should do. When the gods of mythology become
incarnate they work in the realm of circumstances; Jesus speaks
only of the man himself, his heart, his character, and seeks only
to make him good.

Here is, therefore, the essential difference: his conception of
evil, and back of that, of course, his conception of man himself.

As we have seen, in the thought of Jesus the evil and the good,
the woes and the blessings of humanity are in man himself; they
are not in externals, but internals; not in circumstances, but in
character. Jesus does not, therefore, dwell upon poverty or wealth,
sickness, or health, enemies or friends, contempt or favor, ser-
vitude or freedom, early death or long life. He is not concerned
about any circumstances whatever that merely determine man's
external life; he is concerned about man himself. If there be any
real good or any real evil the good and the evil are inside, not outside the man.

Let us note too, Jesus never places man's moral evil, which is
the one evil he recognizes, in mere ignorance of truth, as if in-
structions and merely changing man's opinions could remedy the
evil; he always places it in that something that alienates man's
love from God, that something that Jesus calls sin, that something that is sin because it antagonizes the pure will of God. And
Jesus teaches that the very constitution of man's nature is such

that no bettering of his external conditions can bring any real help whatsoever; that so long as man is out of harmony with God there can be for him, neither in this world not the next, any real good. This he meant in the question that makes a man outweigh a world: "What shall it profit a man if he gain the whole world and lose his own soul?"

Jesus took very great pains to teach men that in themselves, and not in their circumstances, was their real evil and their real good. He used almost every form of speech to teach them to think of a man as a man, and not as the sport of circumstances.

For poverty Jesus did not care; for wealth he had no respect. The story of the barn-builder gives us his solemn judgment upon a man who achieved very great worldly success; who was what most men long and strive to be—rich and great. But he was a man out of harmony with God—rich in purse, bankrupt in soul. Jesus, in the face of all human opinion, plainly calls such a man "a fool."

The drama of the rich man and Lazarus turns the light of both worlds upon the question of man's chief and only good, and emphasizes, by the despair of the prince in hell, his verdict upon the case of the prosperous and self-satisfied barn-builder, in whose thoughts and plans neither his own soul nor the God who made him had any place.

Always—whether speaking of his own personal work or in instructing his disciples as to their work—Jesus looks to bettering men, not their conditions. He did not care for conditions, except as they connected men with influences that made them good or evil; he cared for men only. Hence he always stressed character and nothing else.

Character, in the teaching of Jesus, is all; it is both test and measure of what a man is, and there is no other test or measure for which man ought to care, for which God does care.

The amazement of comfortable and cultured Nicodemus shows us that these ideas of Jesus were not borrowed from the men of his time and race.

Summing up what is here presented as to the conception of Jesus had of his mission to men, a conception as unique as his own character: only one thing he hated and sought to destroy—sin; only one thing for man and sought to bestow—goodness.

Only one thing his true disciples hate—sin; only one thing is worth striving, living and dying for—goodness: which is another name of Christ-likeness.

10

THE MAGNITUDE OF THE END HE PROPOSED AND SET ABOUT

Let us now consider briefly the magnitude of the work Jesus proposed to do as the end of his mission to men.

It is the baldest commonplace to say the work Jesus proposed to accomplish transcends all the dreams of the boldest imagination.

It is a deep offense that once, at St. Helena, Napoleon contrasted the work Jesus proposed to do with the dreams that he and Alexander and Julius Caesar had indulged of world-changing conquests. It is no great thing that selfish, ambitions, and gifted men have dreamed of conquering what we call the world by force. Caesar, Alexander, Mohammed, Napoleon, even poor wild El Mahdi of the desert, may dream such dreams. But what are such dreams when we think of Jesus and the work he proposed to do and set himself to do?

We do not like to think of the dreams of ambition, the loftiest that ever dared or planned a world-wide scheme of conquest, when we are listening to Jesus concerning his mission to men. Jesus speaks of the conquest of all nations, not as they then were, but of all nations for all times. It is nothing less and nothing else than the moral and spiritual re-creation of the human race, the absolute conquest of the love of men's hearts for time and eternity.

Say what men may of Jesus, It was worth dying, in shame

and agony, upon a Roman cross to have had such thoughts, even for one moment. No mere man ever had such thoughts, could originate such thoughts, or for long hold such thoughts in his grasp. The end Jesus proposed to himself is as far above the noblest thoughts of the noblest men as the splendors of the midnight heavens are above the cheap glitter of a toy-shop.

The thought of saving a race was as extra-human and superhuman as the thought of the universe; the saving of a race, the saving of one man, is as far beyond man's power as the creation itself.

We cannot grasp the conception Jesus had of the work he came to do; it makes us dizzy when we contemplate it steadily; it is like trying to realize the distances of the fixed stars. Its splendor blinds us; it is like looking at the unclouded sun.

No one, whatever may be his opinion of Jesus or attitude toward him, can question that he believed absolutely in the success of the work he proposed to accomplish. His plans embrace the entire race of man and require eternity for their consummation, but he speaks of these stupendous things with the perfect assurance and simplicity of a little child: "And I, if I be lifted up, will draw all men unto me."

It were hard to say which is most unlike a mere man: the character of the work he proposed to do, the magnitude of it, the unhasting zeal with which he set about it, or his absolute confidence, calmness, and simplicity of manner in telling men about it.

It is impossible to write worthily on such a theme. Let us, if only for a moment, try to see how unlike a mere man it is.

Jesus considers the sources of man's misery and the nature of his remedy. It is all open, clear, and certain to his thoughts. He has not the least possible doubt that he has gone to the root of the subject and absolutely knows it all. What has confounded all human thinkers is the sunlight to his vision. When the strongest and best of mean tries to mine into the depths of man's nature and misery he labors heavily and breather hard, like a diver in his coat of mail down in the deep sea. When a man attempts to tell what he thinks he sees in the shadows from which he cannot escape, while meditating these difficult and to him impossible themes, he is in sore travail for words; utterance is heavy and confused. But Jesus makes no effort to grasp the truth; his thoughts are clear and complete to him; his language simple and clear to us. It is like this: "Out of the heart proceed evil thoughts." Therefore, there must be, not reformation only, but change. "Ye must be born again," is his first word to Nicodemus and to all who come to him.

There is another thought to be considered at this point in taking note of characteristics which difference Jesus from men. A mere man discovering in his reflections the abysmal depths of man's spiritual malady, a mere man clearly comprehending, as no man ever yet comprehended, the evil of sin, would be crushed by despair. Many good men, seeing but a little way into this darkness, have been made mad by what they saw. Where it is not morbid sentiment or philosophic pay this is the origin of pessimism.

There is nothing of this in Jesus. He saw it all; is uttermost deeps were open to his eyes; but he faces the trouble with infinite calmness. He announces a remedy adequate to the evil. He speaks to a weary and sin-stricken race: "Come unto me, all ye that labor and are heavy laden, and I will give you rest. Take my yoke upon you, and learn of me; for I am meek and lowly in heart; and ye shall find rest unto your souls. For my yoke is easy and my burden is light."

And this is what he offers to a sinning and troubled world. He says he will change men, make them new and good, make them well again.

But there are no lunatic airs, common to dreamers and enthusiasts. No mere man could think such thoughts and earnestly say such things without lunacy. But there never was such perfect mental and spiritual equilibrium as we see plainly in Jesus. He speaks of the moral conquest of the entire race; he asks for the perfect love of men, that he may save them from all evil by saving them from their sins; he speaks of his work as comprehending time and eternity; he offers to the faithful immortality and eternal life. And his calmness of spirit is absolute; his simplicity of manner is perfect.

11

NEVER MAN PLANNED LIKE THIS MAN

What are we to say of the means which Jesus proposes to use for the accomplishment of his vast and unheard-of ends?

I say broadly, and with certain assurance, Jesus proposes none of the means which mere men would use; of the sort they have always used. His plans and methods are utterly unlike the plans and methods of men, except as they have learned most imperfectly from him in humble and earnest efforts to do his will. The methods that mere men trust in—always trust in—he will have none of.

Jesus utterly excludes mere force. His symbol is not a sword; it is a cross. He said, "He that taketh the sword shall perish by the sword."

Some weak thinkers or insincere men have tried to fasten on Christianity the guilt of barbarous cruelties, and many wicked and horrible deeds, perpetrated by ignorant or wicked men in the holy name of Christ. Bad men, in the darkness of ignorance and in the malignity of sin, have used his name to force their brothers to think their thoughts. The rack for Galileo was an evil thought and a wicked method of bad and ignorant men. But Jesus does not tolerate force in carrying on his work, nor persecution of any sort whatsoever.

On one occasion two of his disciples, John and James, were offended because a Samaritan village did not offer hospitality to Jesus and his friends. Then said the brothers, "Lord, wilt thou that we command fire to come down from heaven and consume them?" They were men, and their method was pure human. What Jesus said to them he says to all: "But he turned and rebuked them, and said, Ye know now what manner of spirit ye are of."

To charge upon Christianity the wicked deeds of those who have violated the teachings of its founder is like charging upon medicine the death of men who, in the name of medicine, have been doctored to their death by impostors.

Force could not do any of his work; it was man's love that he sought; and love cannot be forced by God or man. Love dies under force. The Caesars use force; it is a man's way. The God-man uses love.

Jesus does not trust in the purchasing power of wealth, or of money, its representative. He hardly spoke of money except to show the danger of it. The love of money he denounced. He taught that greed of money is debasing. Getting to heaven, for a rich man, is like a camel's passing through the eye of a needle— only "harder." The only rich man who volunteered discipleship turned sorrowfully away when told to sell his estates and give the proceeds to the poor. Jesus warns his disciples with gracious vehemence of the folly and danger of laying up treasure upon earth. Personally he had no concern about wealth, except to warn his disciples of the terrible spiritual dangers that lurk in riches. He provides no treasure for carrying on his work. He taught that the love of money is the source of more moral evils than any other thing in the world.

It is a man's way to bribe and buy favor and success. Satan believes in the power of money absolutely. To Jesus himself the devil offered the submission of the world if he would only pay him allegiance.

Men of our time will not believe what Jesus says upon these subjects, and their prompt rejection of his doctrine is evidence enough that in rejecting from his plans the power of money to buy influence he did not plan like a man. For money, as money, Jesus felt only contempt. He taught that wealth held for its own sake, or used only in selfishness, shows its possessor to be a "fool;" that it both degrades and damns. In his view it can in one way only be even honorable to be rich—to use riches unselfishly and usefully. Even then it is dangerous.

In his day, as they do now, men of the world reviled his doctrine; "the Pharisees, who were covetous, derided him."

For the teachings of Jesus concerning money and its right uses few, even of those who claim to be his disciples and friends, have perfect respect. He seems to them to be "visionary" in his views, and his words seem to be "unbusinesslike." A man says to himself, "Jesus says money is dangerous to my soul; he tells me that I am only a steward holding money in trust, and that I must give it away to those who need. I cannot carry on business on his plan; I will risk my plan."

Such a man does not believe what Jesus teaches; unless one should so far qualify the statement as to say—unless it be that gold has so blinded his eyes that he does not understand what the plain words of the Master really mean.

From his method Jesus excludes diplomacy, the art of playing one selfishness against another. "Let your communication be, Yea, yea; Nay, nay; for whatsoever is more than these cometh of evil." His disciples must, indeed, be "wise as serpents and harmless as doves;" but they must live the truth. Deception is abhorrent to him. The Talleyrands understand and use diplomatic arts. The "Berlin Conference" is a modern instance; it illustrates a man's method. Not necessarily a bad method, but a man's.

Consider a phrase we see every day in the papers, "The balance of power in Europe." See how the "great powers" and the small ones give themselves to all manner of intrigues, using wily statecraft to circumvent, deceive, coerce, hold their own, or rob their weaker neighbors, or by combination reduce the stronger ones.

Many well-founded complaints have been brought against "priest-craft," which is state craft in church circles. Its crimes, by the ill-informed and the evil-disposed, have been laid at the door of Christianity. No charge can be more unjust; it is as unjust as to blame Jesus with the treachery of Judas.

Priest-craft is an invention of men; it has no more place in the plans of Jesus than state-craft; he considers neither, except as he may overrule them and force them against their nature into his service, so that the cunning as well as the "wrath of man shall praise him."

What is called the "Church" is not synonymous with "kingdom of heaven." Men of worldly temper may within church circles do their own work; they do not do Christ's work by diplomatic arts.

Jesus not only excludes appeal to all forms of selfishness, he antagonizes them to the death. His first and last word, his ultimatum, is, "If any man will be my disciple, let him deny himself, and take up his cross daily and follow me." His first word is a challenge to surrender the stronghold of self-will. Till surrender is complete there can be no peace. A mere man would be counted insane—and justly enough—to talk of advancing any little scheme of improving things about him in any such way—and because it is so utterly unlike a man's way.

Jesus offers no inducement to mere self-interest. He promises absolutely nothing of the things the world is in sore travail and anxiety to secure. He does not promise pleasure, or honor, or fortune, or power, or health, or long life. He does say God will see to it that true Christians shall have what is good for them. But in many ways he makes plain that "what is good for them" will often include what the world calls evil.

Jesus nowhere so much as seems to think of what men of the world call good; the things they strive for so, and give their time and strength and lives to gain.

It is an utter mistake to suppose that Jesus offers worldly prosperity as a reward for duty, a premium on piety. Those who try to read this meaning into an apostle's writings misread him; it is against all his teaching. It is true, doubtless, as Paul says, "Godliness is profitable unto all things, having the promise of the life that now is and of that which is to come." But "the promise of the life that now is" cannot, in the kingdom of Jesus, mean worldly things; it means goodness, God's peace in man's soul, Christlikeness in man's heart here and now. Undoubtedly religion makes this a better world, but not because it makes man richer, but purer.

If we believe in Jesus and in his work in the world at all we may, if we wish, find out what he meant by what has followed. It is true that the religion that makes men good restrains them and protects them from the follies and sins that waste energy and squander fortune; but it is utterly misleading and confusing to try to read into the words of Jesus the idea that he appeals to any mere selfish interest by promising fortune to the good. It is like making worldly riches the reward of meekness and long life the premium on obedience to parents.

Some very rich people have been deeply religious, but in spite of their wealth. It is as Jesus said, "All things are possible with God." It was he also who said, "How hardly shall they that have riches enter into the kingdom of God." But Christ's best ones have not succeeded in this world according to money or other such gauges.

If the work of Jesus—who excludes from his plans force and the cunning of diplomacy, who denounces all selfishness and ignores all self-interest, who demands absolute self-surrender at the very outset—is to abide in the world, is to succeed, then it must go against the tide, and not with it.

At one time Jesus seemed to think his hearers might possibly misapprehend him, and he told them plainly that poverty, trouble, sorrow, persecutions in this world, awaited them if they followed him. And he told them plainly, also, that if they would have any part in him and with him they must flinch at nothing—that they must die if need be. When they did understand him "many went back from following him." And many are joining their company to this day.

What he said to the young ruler he said to all; nay, says to us all today: "The foxes have holes; and the birds of the air have nests, but the Son of man hath not where to lay his head." And we do him the deep dishonor of believing that he spoke the words of mere sentiment! He could only mean by his words to the rich young man, "Come with me and welcome; I will help you, I will save you; but for this world I can promise you nothing." He himself was always a poor man, and his poverty was not an accident in his manner of life. There never was a man too poor to be a friend to Jesus, never a man so rich that he could find special favor in those eyes that were "single" and "full of light."

Jesus could not have offered holiness to men as the chief good of man, with worldly blessings as a reason for being good; it would have spoiled the Gospel. He never promised that his disciples should be better off in this world than he was. He asked them one day, "Shall the servant be above his lord, the disciple above his Master?"

But we explain all this away.

Jesus was not indulging sentiment when he taught his disciples that following him meant a self-renunciation that would brave all things. He distinctly told them to expect persecutions and tribulations. And some persuade themselves that he was speaking only for those who were then his disciples; that such ideas do not fit civilized times and countries. An apostle, being a mere man, might well enough give his "judgment" as to what best suited an existing condition of life and society; but Jesus, who belongs to all times, speaks no word of simply local and temporary significance and importance.

It was so certain that suffering and persecution of some sort would follow fidelity that Jesus gave his disciples and all who should come after them a test by which they might judge of their personal fidelity to him: "Woe unto you when all man shall speak well of you." Can we imagine that Jesus did not mean such words for all men, of all times and countries?

He knew how his friends would need to stand firm, and how fearful the pressure of temptation would be to deny him.

He told them they would "for his sake" be "brought before kings," and that "some of them would be killed." But he told them not to be afraid; they were to fear God and no other whatever.

One day Jesus was urging his disciples to be faithful and courageous in proclaiming his whole truth to the world, and thus he encouraged and exhorted them: "And I say unto you, my friends, Be not afraid of them that kill the body, and after that have no more that they can do. But I will forewarn you whom ye shall fear: Fear him, which after he hath filled hath power to cast into hell: yea, I say unto you, Fear him."

Instead of trusting in any wise to self-interest Jesus demands its crucifixion. When he says, "If any man will be my disciple, let him deny himself and take up his cross daily and follow me;" when he demands self-renunciation absolute; when he says that no interest possible in this world—whether houses, lands, father, mother, brother, sister, child, or wife—must come between him and his disciples; when he raises a cross by his own upon which selfishness must die, he stands apart from all men. His method is not a man's. His plans are as different from a man's as the end he proposed is above a man's thought and different from it.

If no man ever spoke like Jesus no man ever planned like him.

In considering further some things in the methods which Jesus adopted for doing the work he proposed to himself we may mention, as different from a man's method, that Jesus excludes from his plans for discipling the world reliance upon mere argument and force on intellect.

Jesus left no room, not the least, for the fanatical superstition that his cause is to be advanced by ignorance. His doctrine furnishes every inspiration for the very highest development of mind; and the best educational work of the world is the outgrowth of Christian institutions.

But Jesus does teach his disciples that they must not, in extending his kingdom, depend upon learning, upon mere force of intellect and argument. If they did this they would fail. So he taught them, and history makes it plain to us that his disciples have failed when they have forgotten his teachings. Alas! that is so easy to pervert great gifts. It seems to be almost as difficult not to trust in great gift of genius as it is to possess great wealth without loving it.

With the end Jesus had in view he could not depend upon mere learning, mental gifts, and force of argument. For the essential trouble is not with men's intellects, but their hearts. It is not that opinions are so wrong; it is that dispositions are so alienated from God. Man needs not a new opinion, but a new love. The task of Jesus was a far harder one than the correction of errors; it was the winning of hearts. Love, is free; men may be convinced against their will, but love consents.

12

Jesus Neither Theologian nor Ecclesiastic

Jesus did none of the things a man would do who proposed to establish and perpetuate any sort of kingdom, or school of beliefs, even in this world.

He established no institutions with formal constitutions. He did not draw up a code—not so much as a system of moral philosophy. He left no "theological institutes," with precise definitions and exact limitations. Some of his true friends have done their best at such work; he did not. Theirs is a man's way; his was not.

He left no formal creed; he never mentioned such a thing; he did not seem to think of it at all. It is so much a man's way to do such things that we are not yet familiar with the idea that Jesus did not. It comes to many with a sudden surprise when they discover that Jesus said not a word about systematic theology, that to many is so precious. In all his words are no "articles of religion;" not a hint of them. He did not so much as put into form a doctrine of his own nature and person. Very often and in many ways he spoke of himself and God, and of his relation to the eternal Father, but he made no definition. Often he spoke of himself, of the Father and of the Holy Ghost, but he said not a word of the "hypostatic union" of three persons in one Godhead; not a word of the "economic relations" of the Holy Trinity.

Some good people, if they chance to read what is here put down, will be so certain in their own minds that Jesus did employ some of the methods of a mere man, in order to preserve his teachings in the world, that they will suspect the writer of irreverence; at least of indifference, if not of something they think less of, in what is said concerning "creeds" and "theologies." They will be in error, as is common with them on such questions; the writer is only stating facts that no man can deny as to what Jesus did and did not do. Some admirable and good people have not yet learned the difference between arguing for their Church and pleading for Christianity; between defending their own notions and expounding the teachings of Jesus. And not a few confound their notions about God with the fact of his existence, as others mistake their theory of inspiration for the divine authority of the Holy Scriptures.

Our way of teaching is a man's way. If it is the best we can do let us be content; if not, let us amend our way. But let us not defend our way by pleading his example; let us follow our way because it is our way, if there be no better reason. Certain it is that the way Jesus took of teaching and perpetuating his doctrines was not a man's way in any respect whatever.

Jesus wrote no book—not a line. He founded no school or other training institution; his three years' loving and painstaking companionship with his disciples was indeed a training, but it was not an institution. This does not mean that his friends should not do such things; it is the only way they can do: but he did not do such things.

He did not so much as establish a Church; the Church grew out of his life as well as out of his teachings; it was compacted by the sympathy of men, women, and little children of common beliefs and hopes; above all, by the sympathy born of a common love for him—this far more, then as now, than by what they understood or believed of his teachings. He left for the government of the Church "no rules of order," no book of "discipline." He ordained no form of church government, "with checks and balances," whatever. All those things may be good, and order in government is necessary; but he did not provide them. He left all such things to the common sense and best judgment, guided by providence and the Holy Spirit, of his disciples. In Church as well as State the principle is this: God ordains the power; he does not prescribe the form; he ordains government, but leaves the form of it to the good sense and personal preferences of those who are to live under it.

All these things we have mentioned here belong to the works and ways of men; they are good or bad as they serve the ends of his kingdom. Moses, though an inspired lawgiver, yet a mere man, gave many forms and prescribed the order of doing many things; Jesus, the divine man, gave none. In nothing is Jesus more unlike men than in his utter disregard of "forms" in the doing of the duties he enjoined. He has no word about forms except the terrible words he used concerning the many forms punctiliously observed by certain Pharisees and hypocrites who were playing at religion. His life was full of worship, but he left not a hint as to any forms or attitudes for devotion. That simplest and most comprehensive of all prayers, "Our Father, who art in heaven," is not a form; he said, "After this manner pray ye." The prayer might take any form of words, or leave all words unsaid. And this prayer he gave his disciples in response to a request for a form. Jesus had no forms; he cared for none.

Nor did Jesus care for the "letter," except as to the danger that good men might make a fetish of it. He said of the "letter, it killeth;" "the Spirit giveth life." The Spirit is every thing, the letter nothing. If we were to use of him the language that fits the case of a man we would feel like saying, Jesus looked upon punctilious eagerness about "forms" and the "letter" as mere child's play, that he scorned such unspiritual folly.

This is certain: the only thing he denounced in a tone that was almost anger was zealous adherence to the form and to the letter, and sanctimonious contentment with this poor substitute for religion when the spirit of worship and service was dead. It will be the plainer to us that his was very far from being a man's way when we remember that, with men, the less of spirit and reality an institution has the more anxious they are about mere form and letter. A spiritually dead man will contend more zealously about the form of a duty than the duty itself. And this is not unnatural; when a Church is dead there is nothing left but form—a body ready for burial.

What terrific words Jesus used in what he said of such things! Let us hear him and try to understand how much he means for us of today:

> "Woe unto you, scribes and Pharisees, hypocrites! for ye pay tithe of mint, and anise, and cummin, and have omitted the weightier matters of the law, judgment, mercy, and faith: these ought ye to have done, and not to leave the other undone.

> "Ye blind guides, which strain out a gnat, and swallow a camel.

> "Woe unto you, scribes and Pharisees, hypocrites! for ye make clean the outside of the cup and of the platter, but within they are full of extortion and excess.

> "Woe unto you, scribes and Pharisees, hypocrites! for ye are like unto whited sepulchers, which indeed appear beautiful outward, but are within full of dead men's bones, and of all uncleanness."

Had Jesus been only a man, conceiving vast plans for propagating his doctrines and perpetuating his kingdom, he would have done all the things he did not do. He would have relied on force, money, diplomacy, argument. He would have considered what human selfishness is, and he would have appealed to it. He would have provided institutions and have founded schools. There would have been a "propaganda" compassing the world in its plans, and his agents would have been drilled in forms and methods after the manner of men. He would, to have been at all like a man in his plans, have left a system of "ethics" or "theology." He would have formulated a "creed"; he would have drawn up a "constitution" with "bylaws" for his Church, stating in terms every principle and providing, according to the foresight given him, for every contingency, as did John Wesley with his Discipline and Legal Hundred. (Can it be necessary to say this illustration is no reflection upon the great and good English reformer, who was a mere man?) He would have set for rigid observance forms and ceremonies of which he had none and prescribed none, not so much as telling men how they were to do in the matter of the sacraments—baptism and the memorial supper.

Mere men always do such things. Jesus did not adopt a man's way in any of his work or plans, unless we except those who have learned of him something of the divine art of doing good to the souls and bodies of men.

13

"Jesus Christ Took the Way of Perishing"

If Jesus was only a man there is another marvelous thing you must have thought of before this time. He talked of a kingdom that was to endure forever, that was to conquer the world, and that was to bind the human race into a body brotherhood; but he made no preparation for a successor. He expected to die early, as he did; he told his disciples, time and again, that he would not be with them long; but he provided for no representative or visible headship when he was gone. The idea of such a representative did not occur in all his thoughts, as it was not intimated in any of his words. Napoleon shows us a man's way in his eager concern for a successor and in the cruel and wicked method he took to secure his ends.

What Jesus did not ordain and require men may use in his work, if their methods be in themselves good, and consistent with the spirit of his kingdom. But what he did not require men must not demand of his free children.

So far as plans are concerned, of a sort recognizable by men as plans—of a sort they will admit who believe he was only a man—there was just one thing he did and commanded. He called about him a few fishermen and other plain people—of what are called by some the "lower classes"—and said in effect: "Go up and down through the earth and tell every body what you have seen me do and what you have heard me say; tell the people of me; tell them to go on repeating the story; tell them to hand it down through the ages, telling it over and over."

These are the very words: "All power is given unto me in heaven and in earth. Go ye therefore, and teach all nations, baptizing them in the name of the Father, and of the Son, and of the Holy Ghost; teaching them to observe all things whatsoever I have commanded you; and lo, I am with you alway, even unto the end of the world."

Mere men, undertaking great and perilous enterprises, conceal from their followers the hardships and perils that await them; they tell them of victories and rewards. So did the Genoese, mustering a crew to help him find a new world. So all mere human leaders do. And no mere man in such a case ever yet clearly saw the difficulty and danger of the undertaking; if men could see clearly the toils and tribulations between them and success they would never enter upon any great and hazardous enterprise. But Jesus saw all the antagonisms that were in his path and, unlike any other leader that ever lived, told his disciples what awaited them. In words like these he spoke to his disciples:

> "Behold, I send you forth as sheep in the midst of wolves: be ye therefore wise as serpents, and harmless as doves. But beware of men: for they will deliver you up to the councils, and they will scourge you in their synagogues; and ye shall be brought before governors and kings for my sake, for a testimony against them and the Gentiles. ...And ye shall be hated of all men for my name's sake: but he that endureth to the end shall be saved. ...The disciple is not above his master, nor the servant above his lord. If they have called the master of the house Beelzebub, how much more shall they call them of his household?...He that taketh not his cross, and followeth after me, is not worthy of me. He that findeth his life shall lose it; and he that loseth his life for my sake shall find it."

Let us think of all this. Such an end to accomplish, such a plan, such a claim, such a promise! If Jesus was only a man this was lunacy, unless we should impeach his sincerity.

Yet with perfect simplicity, perfect composure, perfect confidence, Jesus relies upon such a plan as this. It is not a man's way at all; it is not only above and beyond a man's way, it is unlike it, foreign to it, and impossible to a mere man.

How do men plan? Read history; look about you. It is easy to find out from books; if you know how to read men it is easier to find out from observation.

Alexander, Caesar, Mohammed, among warriors and conquerors; Richelieu, Macchiavelli, Jefferson, Hamilton, Disraeli, Bismarck, among statesman and the men who know state-craft; the fathers and popes, Ignatius Loyola, Luther, Calvin, Wesley, among churchmen—these show us the methods of men. Studying the lives of those mentioned here and of others of their order we will find plans many and diverse—wise and foolish, good and bad—but they show a man's way.

If you wish something more like a parallel consider the plans of those who fastened what is called Buddhism, or Confucianism, upon hundreds of millions. Or consider Mohammedanism. In these systems we see the handiwork of men. The authors of these systems recognize the ordinary influences that determine men's conduct and use them with rare human skill. These employ agencies that Jesus repudiates; they appeal to motives that he ignored; offer inducements that he utterly denied; these planned as men plan in all they did. What Pascal says, in effect, in comparing Christ and Mohammed, we may say of Christ and any other founder of a religion: "If Mohammed took the way of succeeding, according to human calculations, Jesus Christ took the way of perishing, according to human calculations."

Never did Jesus look to using the strongest drifts in human nature to secure his ends; his ends required him to arrest and reverse these drifts. He was not ignorant of the forces locked up in human nature; no man ever so deeply read the heart, so absolutely "knew what was in man." As no other who ever taught men the truth Jesus knew the force of the torrent that bore down upon him—the Niagara his cause had to ascend.

If Jesus was only a man how happened it that the methods he adopted are as unlike the methods of men as the end he sought is unlike the end that any man ever yet proposed to himself? How happened it that in his plans he did every thing that a man would not do, and nothing—all history being witness—that a man would do?

These pages are not written for exhortation; but would it not be better every way, for the cause they stand for, if his friends studied the plans of Jesus more and their own plans less?

Placing ourselves, in imagination, in the company of those few faithful friends, men and women—who were of the humble and obscure people—among those who received his command to "disciple all nations," let us look about us and consider what are our prospects of success.

What predominant influence in the world is friendly to the cause of our Lord and Master? The only people who believe in the Lord God have crucified Jesus. The Romans are masters not only in the holy city but in all the world we know, and the Roman power has just sanctioned the death of Jesus. The Greeks still give philosophy and art to the world, but there is not among the Greeks sympathy with the teachings and work of Jesus. No people befriend his cause; no hand is stretched out to his disciples; the world is against his cause, and for his sake against us, his disciples.

Looking at it all as man might, was there then a single human probability that the cause represented by the crucified Galilean would have the least place in history? That it would abide among men for a single generation? If Jesus was only a man could any thing conceivable by the human mind be more impossible than the realization of the dream (if he was only a man it was but a dream) of this man of Galilee, crucified like a felon?

No wonder certain men, while Jesus was yet among them, "laughed him to scorn."

14

His Grasp Upon Mankind

So far we have been studying the character and work of Jesus as he is presented in the evangelists, just as we might study any other character of that period. We have not yet considered Jesus as he now affects the world—a presence and force of our own times.

When the scientists proved the indestructibility of matter, when they discovered the doctrine of the conservation of energy, showing us how the coal measures, that warm millions of homes and drive the machinery of land and sea, are but stored-up sunbeams of untold ages gone, they showed us that through all her wonderful changes Nature loses none of her substance. In this splendid formulation of natural law the scientists have done a secondary but more important service; they have given us a symbol from things material, an illustration of a law of the higher sphere. Nothing is ever lost in the spiritual world.

A thought with life and truth in it, once set going, can no more be lost than a drop of water falling on the fields can be lost. Professor Harrison, of England, is right in his doctrine of posthumous immortality, as far as it goes. He sees part of a truth and states it well. Whatever force there may be in any human life abides in human life. We may not be able to trace it, as we may not trace the identical dew-drop that glittered on the grass this morning and that, exhaled by the rising sun, has now disappeared from our view, but not from existence.

It may well be that the influences that have conspired in shaping our lives—in making us what we are today—have in some way come to us from many thousands of lives. In a true sense Moses, David, Paul, Socrates, Plato, Augustine, Shakespeare, Bacon, Milton, Luther, Calvin, Wesley, with many others—our parents and teachers above all—all these, and, it may be, myriads more unnameable, live in us today. This is what Froude meant when he wrote of Martin Luther, "No man of our times is what he would have been but for Luther." This is true because Luther's life so enters into the influences of our times that no man ever brought into relations with him could escape that influence.

And few have escaped it; none of the European nations, none of the nations that have been brought into any sort of relations with Christianity and the civilizations that have grown out of it; few, if any, of what we call heathen nations; for the influences of Luther's life and doctrines are in the missionary movement of our times, that now promises to do for these nations what the coming of Christianity did for Europe, Eastern Asia, and Northern Africa in the first centuries of our era—so changed them as to make a new epoch in history; we might say, a new world.

What is true of such a man as Luther is true in a measure—less extensive it may be, less real it cannot be—of every life that has gone before us, and that has, in any way, entered into our own.

It would be easy to offer illustrations. Consider Francis Bacon—perhaps Roger Bacon still more—in relation to the scientific methods of our times. Think of Shakespeare, not in poetry only, but in all literature; or of Kant, Spinoza, Locke, in philosophy; Calvin, Wesley, and the rest, in theology and moral reforms. Or think of the artists and inventors, the great soldiers and statesmen. You may easily make out a very long list of names of human lives that, going before us, now live in us. The list will show names that stand for diverse and antagonistic elements; but all these enter into our lives, just as, to return to our illustration from the world of waters, the water pure from the clouds, sparkling in mountain springs, foul and reeking from swamps and all manner of ugly places, enters, it well may be, into the consistent elements of the dew-drop that reflects the sun upon each grass-blade in the fields.

It is nothing peculiar to the life of Jesus of Nazareth that his influence should abide in human history. Every human life, the humblest and unworthiest, so abides. But the influence of Jesus is different from that of other men. I am not now speaking of degree, but kind. As this method of thinking, of teaching; as the work he proposed to do and as the plans he adopted difference him from mere men, so does the history of the influence that flowed out from him into life and so made modern civilization, so does the character of his influence now difference him from men.

It would carry us too far for the design of these discussions to enter now into the subject of the relation of Jesus to the history of his era. Our calendar intimates the extent and power of that influence; we count time from his birth; this is 1889 AD That influence has entered into whatever has made the world of our times. The history of this influence is the history of the Christian era. We will consider the influence of Jesus, as it may be a matter of observation and consciousness.

Consider the power of the teachings of Jesus upon the human conscience. This is to me a growing wonder. Other men's words stimulate the conscience to a degree, but only when they echo his or approach harmony with them. This is so strangely true that no words of any teacher stir the conscience—except to protest—that antagonize and contradict Jesus. There is no risk of exaggeration or dogmatism here; it is perfectly safe and perfectly fair to say no doctrine of God or man, of rights and wrongs, that repudiates or denies what Jesus teaches, has any power over the human conscience. Other words and doctrines may quicken the intellect and dominate it; may excite the imagination and stir the emotions; but if they are contrary to his doctrines and his life they have no grasp upon the moral side of man.

It is easy to make the experiment and to make it conclusively. Read books that contradict his doctrines—that seek to overthrow them. If you read with candor I am not afraid for you to read what his fiercest enemies say. Take Voltaire, where he ridicules the Bi ble; Paine, in that very misnamed pamphlet, The Age of Reason; Hume, in his speculations concerning providence, miracles, inspiration, and the whole agnostic literature of our day. These writings do not take hold upon the conscience except as they may weaken or paralyze it; they do not strengthen any purpose to do right, confirm any sense of personal obligation, invigorate any will for right doing. Make the experiment with any words of men that contradict or repudiate Jesus, the lightest and weightiest, the silliest and subtlest; mere platform declamations or the sober scientific worship of materialism that knows no spirit—man, angel, or God. Do any of them stir our sense of obligation to high duty? Do any of them make our perception of duty clearer? Our love of virtue stronger? Our hatred of evil intenser? All who have made the experiment may answer for themselves.

I do not say that only the words of Jesus take hold upon the conscience; this would not be true. There are passages in Seneca, in Epictetus, in Socrates, in Plato, in Confucius, in the words of many ancient sages and modern teachers, that do stir the conscience. Your Shakespeare will furnish many illustrations. So will George Eliot, Hawthorne, and very many other writers. But these things I do say with perfect assurance:

1. No words or teachings of any writer or teacher, of any age, that antagonize or repudiate the words of Jesus have power over the conscience.

2. Those words and teachings of men who never knew Jesus—as Socrates, Confucius, and other such men—that most affect the conscience are those words and teachings of theirs most in harmony with the doctrines and character of Jesus. All light is good, but that which is nearest sunlight is best.

3. The words and teachings of those who do know Jesus, that most powerfully affect the conscience, are those that most perfectly echo his words.

Furthermore, this is true: The words and teachings of Jesus not only stir the conscience as no others do; they illuminate the conscience. Others may affect the sensibility of conscience to a degree, but leave it in the shadows as to the very rights and wrongs of things. The words of Jesus—once their meaning is understood—as they apply to any concrete case of rights and wrongs, not only awaken the sensibility of conscience so that the feeling of obligation to do right and avoid wrong is most pronounced and unmistakable, but this also is true: the light which his words pour on the question in consideration makes transparent what the right thing is and what the wrong thing is.

There is something here that defies analysis, something that will not be held in logic forms. Take any doctrine Jesus taught and exemplified. It may be about truth, honesty, chastity, charity. Read it, see what it means, apply it to your case, and conscience says, "Amen" to it, and upon the instant. Conscience receives it as the reason receives an axiom. Given the facts, you need only to apply his tests, and that instant you not only suppose, not only think, you know what is your right and your wrong in the case. If there were no other reason, herein there is reason enough to follow the Man of Galilee wherever he leads.

I urge upon you for your use in the tests that await you, as a method of finding out rights and wrongs and determining duty, what I have tried under many conditions of life and action; a most simple principle of action—one that has never for one moment failed me or left me in doubt. It is worth more than all reasonings, than all books of casuistry, than all advices of friends; nay, it is better than mere praying as if for some new light or other revelation than that which has come to enlighten every man that cometh into the world. It is to ask, "What does Jesus teach here? What would he say if he were here to speak? What would he do if this were his case?"

Blunders of judgment, many and grievous; failures in living up to the light that the Master gives, more grievous than any blunders of judgment—these things I confess to sorrowfully and with bitter shame; but for the truth's sake, my conscience' sake, and my Lord's sake, this much I must say, and I cannot say less: never have I asked, "What would he do?" but that the light has shined resplendent and all-revealing, and the right and the wrong stood out clear, sharp, as when electric lights shine about us, and I knew what I ought or ought not to do.

At this point we may recur a moment to what was, in part, considered heretofore: the fullness, the completeness of his teachings difference him from all others.

There is not in any other teacher such a statement of principles that you cannot find outside their teachings one single ethical principle that they have not taught. Other teachers give us many principles of ethics; does any of them give all? Jesus does, though he wrote no book and elaborated no system; though we have but few of his words recorded. What I ask is this: Is there in any teacher of any nation one single principle of rights and wrongs that the suffrage of the race could approve, that Jesus does not teach? Is there one single principle of Jesus as to rights and wrongs that the suffrage of good men can condemn as false? Men may, indeed, reject his teachings, and oppose them with bitterest hate, but which one of them—the least or the greatest—can they show to be immoral, wrong?

As all colors are potentially contained in the pure white light, and as the composition of all colors produces the pure white light, so the teachings of Jesus contain in principle all the forms of ethical truth that were ever in the minds of men. But here the analogy fails. All the ethical truth that all others have taught when brought together fails to make the sum total of his teachings; some colors are lacking in them; together they do not make the pure white light of the gospels.

15

WHAT HE CLAIMS AND DEMANDS

There is a fact, personal to Jesus, that not only enters vitally into this argument, but more than anything else explains the power of his words on the conscience: what was considered in another relation in the outset—the perfection of his own character; his sinlessness: his absolute purity.

A perfect doctrine will no doubt affect the conscience, but a perfect doctrine uttered by one who lives a holy life has tenfold the power of the mere statement of doctrine. And it is not simply that the hearer recoils from a doctrine stated by an inconsistent or insincere man because he is inconsistent and insincere, but such a man cannot so much as utter the truth in its fullness; he cannot conceive the truth in its completeness.

When Jesus utters a truth it lays hold upon the conscience and life not simply because it is the truth, but because he is the "Truth and the Life." His conscience goes with the word and it enters into our conscience. It was this quality in him, more than aught else, that led his hearers, when the Sermon on the Mount was ended, to "wander at his doctrine, for he taught them as one having authority." It is living a truth more than learning about a truth that gives the teacher authority.

An illustrative incident may help us here. The late Mr. Wray was a Baptist missionary in India. He was a man of known consistency of religious character. A child who knew him well was asked the question: "What is holiness?" A man would have done as so many do with lamentable failure, attempted a "definition;" the child answered "Holiness is the way Mr. Wray lives." The child was nearly, if not quite, at the bottom of the subject.

The learner in the school of Jesus may find here a truth of first importance. It is twofold: 1. The best way to learn more truth is to live the truth he does know. 2. The only way to rightly teach any truth in morals, in things spiritual, is to live it. Religion, like science, believes in experiment and teaches by facts. The incarnate truth is the truth that has life in it. It is said with reverence, but with confidence, Jesus teaches what spiritual life is more by living it than by his words. His life expounds his doctrine, and without his life we could not understand his teachings.

Try the principle by any test of him. For example, he teaches us that forgiveness is a duty and that revenge is a sin. What does he mean? What he did. You remember his last prayer: "Father, forgive them; they know not what they do." He teaches us to love our enemies. What does he mean? What he did; always blessing them when he could. He teaches that we best serve God by doing good to men, and that the best proof and only proof of loving God is in loving men. What does he mean? What he did. He was always doing good. And so his life expounds his teachings, and is the one safe and true commentary upon his words.

Contemplate that life for a moment. Begin at Bethlehem and follow him to Bethany, where, it is said, he ascended to heaven. That life is blameless, flawless. He did not lack abuse, denunciation, defamation, persecutions. Men called him a drunkard and a glutton because he was not an ascetic; they said he "had a devil" because they could not understand how any man would do a thing only because it was right. Some called him a lunatic; "he is beside himself," they said, because he was unworldly, was what they considered "unbusinesslike," because they, with their selfishness and pride, could not imagine themselves as he did unless they had lost their reason. Many hated him then, as they do now, because he was, as he is, in the way of their self-seeking and their sins. Bad men cannot be at rest where he is.

No wonder the perfect teaching of a blameless man has power upon the human conscience. To this hour good men indorse Pilate's verdict; bad men can find no error in it.

When we look more closely into his innermost character we will find qualities that difference him from mere men broadly and unmistakably. We see in him no fault that we can name as attaching to his life; but we do see in him two manifestations of all others most marvelous and out of the range of mere human life. 1. There does not appear in him any, the very least, consciousness of fault. 2. In his religion there is no effort.

Now these things appear in no others who are sincere—who know what they are and what goodness is. The best men and women are conscious of faults, and the best men are most conscious of them. If a man should say, "I am faultless," we would question his sincerity, his sanity, or his knowledge of words, or his conception of goodness. And we would be right. No sane man, with any high ideal of goodness and knowing the meaning of words, ever yet used of himself words that fit only Jesus.

It is like a true artist's ideal: the better artist he is the less he satisfies his own conception in what he does; so in religion, the saintliest most realize the distance between them and the Christ. A unbeliever has said that Mary at the sepulcher idealized him, and so made Christianity possible! He supposed he had accounted for the most stupendous fact of all time. Why is it that only Jesus has become the highest ideal that ever filled the human soul? That nineteen centuries have added nothing to him—taken nothing from him?

As to men, religion is war with nature. Saint Paul teaches us. It was his experience; the holiest men best understand this and most frankly confess it. Paul's writings are full of terms that illustrate religion from agnostic struggles. When Jesus himself urges men to seek the life of religion he says, "Strive to enter in at the strait gate." The word translated strive is the Greek form of our word of pain and conflict—agonize.

But the religion of Jesus was effortless; there was never in his heart antagonism to goodness. His religion shines like the sun because it is full of light; it is a going forth from fountains that, in his inmost soul, were in spontaneous and perpetual play. He did have conflicts, but with the evil and that was without him; there was none in him.

The story of his temptation does not at all militate against this statement. The force of the attack from without he felt, for it is said, "He suffered being tempted." But when we read the story we feel that it was not only right for him to resist, but natural. We see so clearly that we never doubt; there is in him nothing in sympathy with the evil to which he was solicited.

What does Jesus say of himself as to these things? What does he claim for himself? He says to Pilate, "I am the truth;" and it does not shock us to hear him say this. He says in one place, "I do always the will of my Father;" and we believe him—not only that he thinks he does, but that he does. In trying to give to his disciples the one true ideal of humanity he says, "Be ye therefore perfect, even as your Father in heaven is perfect." Then he offers himself as an example to the human race, and we are satisfied that he is what he says, for we can "find no fault in him." And with it all we recognize perfect sincerity, simplicity, humility. If a mere man were to say such things to us we would despise him; the scorn of the world would drive him from the presence of men. But he says such things and we feel that it is right; it is the truth; he is what he says.

In the same way we feel that he is entitled to make upon us the most tremendous claims for human service, devotion, and love ever put into words. He says, "If any man will be my disciple, let him deny himself and take up his cross daily, and follow me." "He that loveth father or mother more than me is not worthy of me." All must be in abeyance to his will. We are to forsake lands, homes, parents, children, wives, all for him. Nothing in the universe must come between him and the loyal, all-sacrificing love of his disciples. He must be first in our hearts; whatever comes between him and our love forfeits all claim upon him. If a mere man made these demands the world would despise him, and the world would be right.

But he sets up other claims of a sort no sincere and sane man, who is only a man, can think of for a moment. He claims the right to forgive sins. His critics were right—assuming him to be only a man. "Why does this man thus speak blasphemies? Who can forgive sins but God only?"

He not only claims, as no other prophet ever did, to represent the eternal Father, but he claims a perfect knowledge of God that no mere man can claim. "All things are delivered unto me of my Father; and no man knoweth the Son but the Father; neither knoweth any man the Father save the Son, and he to whomsoever the Son will reveal him." The night before he died he said to his disciples: "Let not your heart be troubled: ye believe in God, believe also in me."

He says in many ways and in many places that he is, in origin and character, more than a man; that he is supernatural. He says, "I and my Father are one." He says that he is divine—that he is God.

If Jesus was only a man such claims cannot be reconciled with his sanity or his sincerity. Augustine was right when he reduced this argument to its last analysis: *"Christus, si no deus, non bonus"*—Christ, if he be not God, is not good.

16

JESUS THE ONE UNIVERSAL CHARACTER

In considering Jesus as he is now in the world, not in the story of the evangelists and in books simply, but in human life, there are other views to be taken. We can take views only; we cannot see all that they indicate.

We must consider more carefully now what we looked at for a moment in the argument that compels us to believe that this character could not have been invented, and that such a personality could not have been a normal outgrowth of Hebrew life: Jesus is a universal character—the one and only universal character that has ever appeared in history, that has ever been described, that has ever had a place in human thought.

There are great differences in men. Some are so narrow and meager of soul as scarcely to have a thought or sympathy beyond the little circle in which they are born, in which they live, and out of which they go utterly when they die. There are lives so localized that men out of their sphere they cannot understand, and that men out of their sphere cannot understand them. For every limited dialect in human speech there are limited thoughts and lives back of it. What do we mean by "provincialism" as applied to a man, or to the people of a State or country? It means limitation. Illustrations are everywhere. Take a Scotch Highlander, an Irishman of some seldom-visited farming region, or, in our own country, a New Englander born and bred, never from home; or a village Georgian, a thorough-going old time Southerner. These men are provincial. They may have admirable and indeed noble qualities, but they are limited in their views, narrow in their sympathies, and by so much they are cut off from the sympathies of their fellow-men of other conditions in life. Savage people show us the extremes of provincialism.

But let us take now our illustration from the loftiest ranges of life. Among the ancients take Plato—broad-minded as any. What is he? Grecian to the core. There was no greater Roman than Julius Caesar. But he was essentially Roman; he was localized by race and country; there was much in him that only a Roman could understand, and therefore much that limited him in his knowledge of the men of other nations.

Come to more modern times. Only a few years ago the Protestant world celebrated the four hundredth anniversary of the birth of Martin Luther. There was enough in Luther to perpetuate his influence through many generations. In every nation where the effect of the Lutheran reformation is felt there was real interest in the celebration of the anniversary of the great German's birth. There was less sympathy with Luther; moreover, more or less understanding of him. There was enough forceful life in Luther to overflow Germany and enrich other lands; yet he was a German, and so not a universal, but a limited, character. And so it is that he means more to Germany than to England, or France, or America. It is not simply that Germans are more interested in him as a patriotic sentiment growing out of national pride in their greatest man; they understand him better than other people can. If he could come back to the world he would understand Germans better than he would other people.

Among great men in civil life take American Washington. Great man though he was, and having in him qualities that all true men recognize and approve, he was yet essentially American. He was also essentially Virginian, and plantation-aristocratic Virginian of his time, and no other.

Take English Gladstone, of living men. Broadminded, well-informed, ripe in wisdom, rich in learning, all-accomplished, he is, it may well be supposed, second to no man of our times in greatness of heart and range of sympathies. But he is English; there is much in him that no foreigner can fully understand, and there is much in any foreigner that Gladstone cannot understand.

Take one more illustration—the man we call "myriad-minded"—the prince of poets, the king of dramatists, William Shakespeare. He could, I think, put himself into the consciousness of a man of a different nation as fully as any man who ever wrote. He is as nearly as one can be "poet of the human race." But it is a mere commonplace of literature to say that many of the best thoughts in his great dramas cannot bear translation into foreign tongues; just as the finest oranges that grow, as travelers tell us, a variety grown in Brazil, cannot bear transportation to other countries. If it be said this is a language difficulty, this itself implies the limitation that goes with mere men. But this does not explain the difficulty of translation altogether; it is in the limitations that characterize men. No foreigner can rightly understand Shakespeare, who was English.

It has been said by some writer: "Shakespeare dramatized the sixteenth century Englishman." He wrote of others; he dramatized the Englishman of his time. He knew him. He did not dramatize the sixteenth century man. There is no character who can be at home in every country; who can stand for the race. Still less did he dramatize the nineteenth century man; genius is not equal to such a forecast. For mere men are not only localized in thought, sympathy, and character, by place, they are, if possible, still more limited by time, the influences that went before them and shut them in while they lived.

But what do we find when we consider Jesus of Nazareth in respect to time and place, blood and country, education and language? This: we do not at all think of him, though we use the words, as Jesus of Nazareth. We do not think of him as a Jew—as an Asiatic even. The Galilean, the Jew, the Asiatic is lost in the man. Circumstances left no such impress upon Jesus as to localize him—as to limit his sympathy—as to mar in the least his all-around, harmonious, perfect humanity.

If translators have thorough language-knowledge the words of Jesus bear translation as no words of men bear it. I do not believe that his thoughts lose any thing, any flavor, any color, by being translated. Where they are properly translated his thoughts mean to an American what they meant to the people who first heard him speak. They produce in men of different races and tongues the same thoughts, excite the same convictions, stir the same sympathies, and lead to the same conclusions about rights, and wrongs, and duties, in every language that has ever repeated them. When these words of Jesus are obeyed they produce the same essential characteristics alike in men of every nation, the most enlightened and the most savage. It does not depend on race, or heredity, or environment; the results in character of receiving and living the Gospel are the same always and everywhere. Whether Greek, or Roman, or Scythian, or Hebrew in the early days of Christianity; whether Caucasian, Asiatic, African today, the man who follows the Christ is transformed into his likeness. No soil, no climate, no time changes the fruit of this tree.

Above all, and least like any mere man, not only do his words mean to us what they meant to his first disciples; he means as much to us. He is to a sinful and penitent woman of our times just what he was to that Mary who kissed his feet in the house of the proud Pharisee. He is to any vile wretch who needs and wants him just what he was to the man full of leprosy, or to him of Gadara. To Marys and Marthas weeping their dead today he means just as much as to the sisters of Bethany. All this agrees with what he said of himself as "the Son of man." Did any other ever have such a conception of himself, of the human race, and of his relation to it? Not one word, not one act of his is shut up to his time or race. Jesus is "the Son of man;" the ideal and universal man, the representative man of the entire race, the brother of every man, woman, and child in the world; loving all and adoringly lovable by all.

17

THE CHRIST,
THE SON OF THE LIVING GOD

What has been set forth concerning the power of the teachings of Jesus to stir and stimulate and enlighten the conscience; what has been said of his own character and life as incarnating, and thereby expounding, making clear and enforcing, his doctrine; what has been suggested concerning the absolute universality of his character, making him brother to every human being and therefore as much to one as to another, all this brings us to speak briefly of a wonderful but very common fact of daily observation and experience, a fact that cannot be dissevered from the character, nature, and personality of Jesus himself: the effect of his doctrines and of himself upon men.

It is not meant that all who are called Christians show these results; that all who are Christians show all these results; that any man or woman who ever was called Christian has shown all the results possible to humanity as the natural sequence of receiving fully the doctrine of Jesus and living up to it. No more than I will plead for counterfeit coins; no more than I would say that all coins that have pure gold in them are of full weight and without alloy of baser metal. But this I do say: we do find, and always find, in those who receive and obey the teachings of Jesus the results he pointed out as following their reception; that the results follow in proportion to the thoroughness with which these teachings are observed; that those who best keep them become most like him, the one blameless and perfect Man.

We will not enter into any theological discussions; we do not touch the metaphysics of the subject; but this may be affirmed roundly and without qualification: those who believe and receive and obey his words are not only changed in their manner of life, they are, so far as we can have any means of judging men, changed in their spirit of life. So it does come to pass in those who keep his words; old things become new, not only in the sphere of action, but also in the sphere of thinking, feeling, willing.

As it seems to me, there can be nothing in this world harder to do than to change, not men's external lives merely, but men themselves. Changing men's hearts is like making worlds.

Who else who ever taught, lived, or died, does this? Does this while among men? Does this, being for nearly two thousand years gone out of the sight and hearing of men? But Jesus works this miracle now, and in men of all races and conditions, civilized and savage, learned and unlearned. And their number is as the sands by the sea-shore and as the stars of heaven for multitude.

Candid thinkers in accounting for Jesus—in characterizing and classifying him—must take account of the effects produced in human character, as well as in human lives, and in human lives because in human character.

The men of science tell us we must take account of facts in forming our conclusions; and they are right. It was Jesus who taught this principle long before Bacon; "By their fruits ye shall know them." In studying Jesus we must take account of those facts in human life which seem to be connected with him.

We have spoken of the change in character—call it by any name or none—that follows obedience to Jesus. In this connection there is another most wonderful thing to be considered. What I am to mention now is, on the mere grounds of common sense and worldly reasoning, the most marvelous and inexplicable of all facts observed among men in relation to any being not with them in visible, tangible form; I refer to the matchless love his true disciples feel toward him, not as a teacher, but as a person.

None can deny it. Who, if Jesus was only a man, can explain it?

No man who knows history, or the world today, will doubt for one moment that millions on millions of human beings—men, women, and little children—have felt and shown for the person of Jesus the most absorbing love; a love that drove out all fear and mastered every other love. Some great teachers and leaders while they were yet in the flesh have had followers and friends who loved them well enough to hazard life for them and to die for them. We can understand the soldier who, on one occasion, when a shell fell close by the first Napoleon, while it was just exploding flung himself between the fatal bomb and his loved chief, and throwing his arms about him died in his stead. But when Napoleon was an exile in St. Helena he complained one day that, among all those he had befriended in the days of his power, there were none to draw sword for him when he was an exile. Who would die for Napoleon now?

There have been thinkers, poets, orators, philosophers, who have enthusiastic admirers who contend for them in the pretty war of words. Shakespeare has as many such admirers as the foremost in all the world. But who loves him—the man—in any such deep, absorbing fashion as untold millions have loved and to now love the Man—Jesus of Nazareth? It surprises you to hear such a question. If Jesus was only a man the question should not surprise. How does it come about that such love as the great army of martyrs and confessors have shown was never felt for any except this Galilean peasant?

There is not now, there never was such love for Buddha or Mohammed. Such love was never professed for the founders of Buddhism or Mohammedanism. Such love was never felt for any person long gone from the midst of men.

This love is not like the fanaticism that fights for one's own idea; it is the love of a person for a person. This love for Jesus has shown itself to be the master love that ever held sway in the human heart. For this love all other loves have been given up—have been crucified.

Do men and women, in their senses, give their strength and life-long service for any other name? Die cheerfully for any other name? Die for one long gone away from them—gone out of the world and, so far as sense and reason know, gone forever? But neither lapse of centuries, distance by separating seas, distances unknown between this world and the world men do not know, or separation by differences of race, cools his love. What the martyrs did in Jerusalem they soon afterward did in Rome, in Alexandria, in every city and country of that age and that part of the world. They did the same thing—died with songs on their lips for this Man of Galilee—in after centuries. So did they in the Middle Ages in every country of Europe. So they have done in our own time in that great island, Madagascar, that has shown in the dark sons of the tropics, whose fathers were heathen idolaters, the overmastering love of men, women, and children, for the Jesus they had never seen; who lived on the other side of the world from them, and taught men how to be saved nearly two thousand years ago. They died in Madagascar as they died in Rome, "the love of Christ constraining them."

And the best people in the world today would so die for him in every country where his word has gone. And this love grows fuller and stronger; Jesus is more in the thoughts and love of men than he ever was before.

If you would in some sense realize the wonder of which we are now speaking, try to imagine such a passion coming into the hearts of millions of men today as would impel them to die with rejoicings for Socrates, or any other born of woman, save the Man who was once a carpenter in Joseph's shop in Nazareth of Galilee. You cannot imagine such a thing. As to Jesus, and love for him, it is not left to imagination; we have history. And we know a great multitude who would gladly die for Jesus now if to them should come the martyr's test.

When Jesus disappeared from the sight of men there was not a human probability that his name would be other than a reproach, till, like any common felon—like the forgotten thieves between whom he died—his name and fate should drop out of the memory of men. Humanly speaking, it was certain that he would never have a solitary follower. No sane man, reckoning on the ordinary probabilities of human motives and action, could have conceived the possibility of a vast body of disciples, ever growing, and pushing on his conquests round the world, holding together through passing centuries, enduring all manner of opposition and bitter persecution, and now, in this year 1889, the master-force of the world; a force that, beyond all cavil, is now the most active, aggressive, and revolutionizing influence ever set going among men.

It could not have been conceived; every dominant power of the world was arrayed against him; there was not a star shining for Jesus if he was only a man.

But Jesus crucified lives on. Around his cross has been the battle-ground of the ages. All that human skill and bitter hate could do has been done to put out the light he kindled on Calvary. But he lives on—lives in men today; single-handed he goes on his conquering way. His servants, because they love him, are pushing his cause in every nation under heaven. As in the old days, in the lands that bordered the Mediterranean, so now among the great pagan nations—in India, China, Japan, Africa, and in the islands of the sea, they are telling the story he commanded them to repeat till he should come again. And, telling it, they are now, as in the days of his first apostles, "turning the world upside down."

In every land his children are building up his kingdom. They die for him, and others take their places; and so the work begun in Jerusalem never ceases. History confirms his promise, "I am with you alway, even unto the end of the world."

Such a character could not have been conceived had not such a life been lived; such a life could not have sprung out of Hebrew soil; no mere man ever new the deepest truths without investigation or taught them without proving them; no mere man ever conceived of such a work as Jesus proposed to himself, and no mere man would have adopted the methods Jesus used; no mere man ever conceived so vast an undertaking as the moral conquest of the race; no mere man ever took such masterful hold upon the conscience, love, and will of mankind.

————————————

What Simon Peter said stands today as the faith of the Church: "Thou art the Christ, the Son of the living God." The great words of St. John stand firm as the teaching of Scripture and the verdict both of reason and history: "The Word was with God, and the Word was God. ...And the Word was made flesh, and dwelt among us, (and we beheld his glory, the glory as of the only begotten of the Father,) full of grace and truth."

The facts of his humanity and of his work and influence in the world forbid us to classify Jesus with men, and the recognition of his divinity alone explains the facts of his humanity. Considered as God-man all is in harmony; miracles take their proper place in the records of his history, and mind and nature, heaven and earth, God and man meet in Jesus, the Christ.

But—if he be only a man—he is such a man as were a thousand times worth dying for and following forever, through time and eternity.

HERITAGE
OF FAITH LIBRARY

The **DeWard Publishing Company Heritage of Faith Library** is a growing collection of classic Christian reprints. DeWard has already published or has plans to publish the following authors:

- A. B. Bruce
- Atticus G. Haygood
- H. C. Leupold
- J. W. McGarvey
- William Paley
- Albertus Pieters
- B. F. Westcott

Future authors and titles added to this series will be announced on our website.

www.deward.com

DEWARD
PUBLISHING COMPANY

ALSO FROM DEWARD PUBLISHING:

Beneath the Cross: Essays and Relfections on the Lord's Supper
Jady S. Copeland and Nathan Ward (editors)

The Bible has much to say about the Lord's Supper. Almost every component of this memorial is rich with meaning—meaning supplied by Old Testament foreshadowing and New Testament teaching. The Lord's death itself is meaningful and significant in ways we rarely point out. In sixty-nine essays by forty different authors, Beneath the Cross explores the depths of symbolism and meaning to be found in the last hours of the Lord's life and offers a helpful look at the memorial feast that commemorates it. 329 pages. $14.99 (PB); $23.99 (HB)

Invitation to a Spiritual Revolution
Paul Earnhart

Few preachers have studied the Sermon on the Mount as intensively or spoken on its contents so frequently and effectively as the author of this work. His excellent and very readable written analysis appeared first as a series of articles in *Christianity Magazine*. By popular demand it is here offered in one volume so that it can be more easily preserved, circulated, read, reread and made available to those who would not otherwise have access to it. Foreword by Sewell Hall. 173 pages. $9.99 (PB)

Hello, I'm Your Bible
Jason Hardin

A practical guide to understanding and applying God's word of truth. Whether you've just been introduced to the Bible, you'd like to get reacquainted with the Scriptures, or you're looking to grow in your ability to help others in their walk of faith, *Hello, I'm Your Bible* can guide you into a deeper relationship with the God behind the living and active word. 156 pags. $9.99 (PB)

Things Most Surely Believed
Forrest D. Moyer

In these 16 brief sermons, Forrest Darrell Moyer has stated with beautiful clarity and simplicity, yet with compelling force, the Christian's "reason for hope" that is in him. He deals with the greatest themes the race has ever known—God, Christ, the cross, sin and redemption, the church, heaven and hell—yet he does it in language that the man in the pew, unskilled in the intricacies of theological vocabularies, can easily grasp. These sermons partake of that same quality which characterized the initial preaching of the gospel by Christ himself, of whom it was said, "and the common people heard him gladly." 142 pages. $9.99 (PB)

The Growth of the Seed: Notes on the Book of Genesis
Nathan Ward

A study of the book of Genesis that emphasizes two primary themes: the development of the Messianic line and the growing enmity between the righteous and the wicked. In addition, it provides detailed comments on the text and short essays on several subjects that are suggested in, yet peripheral to, Genesis. 537 pages. $19.99 (PB)

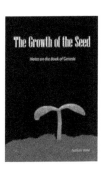

Churches of the New Testament
Ethan R. Longhenry

Have you ever wondered what it would be like to be a Christian in the first century, to meet with the church in Philippi or Ephesus? *Churches of the New Testament* explores the world of first century Christianity by examining what Scripture reveals about the local churches of God's people. It examines background information about the geography and history of each city, as well as whatever is known about the founding of the church there. Centuries may separate us from the churches of the New Testament, but their examples, instruction, commendation, and rebukes can teach us today. 150 pages. $9.99 (PB)

For a full listing of DeWard Publishing Company books, visit our website:

www.deward.com

CPSIA information can be obtained
at www.ICGtesting.com
Printed in the USA
LVHW041338280623
750573LV00005B/86

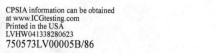